Udo Kultermann

Art and Life

Translated by John William Gabriel

Praeger Publishers

New York · Washington

BOOKS THAT MATTER

Published in the United States of America in 1971
by Praeger Publishers, Inc., 111 Fourth Avenue,
New York, N.Y. 10003

Library of Congress Catalog Card Number: 76-145535

Printed in Germany

Contents

"With the help of the superego, the ego,
in a way still unkown to us, draws from the experiences
of ancient times past collected in the id."

Sigmund Freud

Introduction

This book is the last in a series of studies on the culture of the 1960s, which includes "New Architecture in the World" (1965), "The New Sculpture" (1968), and "The New Painting" (1969). Its purpose is to show the relationship of this culture to reality, or, in a broader sense, the function of art in our epoch. The accents have changed in all facets of life and art—from the abstract to the concrete, from the isolated to the all-encompassing—and the all-encompassing is reality itself.

Ludwig Wittgenstein's insight came early: "even if all conceivable scientific questions could be answered, the problems of living would not have been touched upon. Of course, then there is no longer any question to be asked—and that, in itself, is the answer." And he concluded, "The stock questions are of no use for a logical examination of these phenomena. Such questions give rise to more of the same, or, more likely, provide their own answers."[1]

Assuming, then, the existence of completely open-ended systems, where there are no definite answers because the data are too disparate, I shall examine forms of art produced in the 1960s that transcend the long-standing boundaries between art and life.[2]

Art cannot be explained, and the question of its essence can be answered only incompletely, just as questions about the meaning of life can never be answered conclusively. Any attempt to formulate answers has to be makeshift; our initial assumption must be that we know nothing. Before I begin, I should make it clear that, for me, life is the sum total of all processes permanently regenerating themselves. The special capacity of the human race

1 Ludwig Wittgenstein, Zettel, Oxford, 1967.
2 Karl R. Popper, The Open Society and Its Enemies, London, 1945; Princeton, N.J., 1950. 7

lies in its ability to conceive of the self and, as one consequence of this, to produce art. Art, seen in this light, is a function of life. Man differs in his forms of expression from all other living things—both plant and animal—in his ability to make art.

Art is the uniquely human stamp put by man on life; it is his way of facing and subduing the world. It is the basic form of communication between men, the most ancient language of ideas, the seed of society. Art is the foundation of human society, the one factor that generates the formation of groups of men who share values and ideals. It represents a new function in life, one that was non-existent until the advent of man. Even the earliest known works of primitive man share with those of contemporary artists the need to ask the questions most central to life: How did the world come into being? Can man survive? John Cage formulates it like this: "Art, instead of being an object made by one person, is a process set in motion by a group of people. Art's socialized. It isn't someone saying something, but people doing things, giving everyone (including those involved) the opportunity to have experiences they would not otherwise have had."[3]

Today we realize that (as far as we can put it into words and check it against reality) life is all-encompassing; it consists of the sum total of all realities that have any bearing at all on our existence. Art is a part of this; or perhaps better, art has an organizing function. Art enables man to organize his life in ways impossible for plants or animals. Art was, is, and will be as long as he exists on this earth a sign of man's emancipation, of his ability to exist in the world in a way completely unattainable for all other forms of life.

Hence it is always a mistake to speak of the "end" of art, the end of a function that has existed as long as man himself. The "death" of art, proclaimed at regular intervals, bears witness only to its prophets' inability to admit that art must be continually redefined.[4] Art, as a phenomenon, remains; every "end" means only a new beginning—an escape from a fixed form, grown petrified through use, into a form more relevant to the times. Art repeatedly regains meaning as a function of continually changing human life, as essentially a "question of life and death." Art never loses its importance to life. It is always necessary. It is man's unique way of confronting his world.

This world, the here and now of our political, social, and psychological situation, includes more than the real and present perceptions registered by our consciousness; it also includes all past forms of the real, even those reaching far back into history. All current impressions, if seen in all their complexity and in perspective, can be traced back to the first and simplest forms of human existence, much farther than Aby Warburg thought—his Mneme or Mnemosyne was bounded by the antique world.[5] The universal

3 John Cage, A Year from Monday, Middleton, Conn., 1967, p. 151.
4 Oto Bihalji-Merin, Ende der Kunst im Zeitalter der Wissenschaft?, Stuttgart, 1969.
5 Udo Kultermann, Geschichte der Kunstgeschichte, Düsseldorf, 1966, pp. 374–83.

chain goes much further back; the more of it we can follow, the more acute is our consciousness of self. This retrospective view of the past as eternal present can stand as a metaphor for intellect penetrating the depths of consciousness. The convolutions of the human brain have become more and more complex with the passage of time; they, just as the ever-deepening labyrinths of the past, represent the interior spaces of time.

If we compare the contingencies of artistic expression today with those of the past, it becomes clear that much of what we see now can be traced back to the beginnings of human development, and that certain behavioral patterns have remained unchanged over thousands of years of history.[6] This is true of both private and public forms of behavior; it is expressed in such disparate rites as birthday parties, marriage ceremonies, and burials; in professional and political conventions, in propaganda, in church and military ceremony, in sport, tourist travel, and daily life in the office men continue to behave— usually without being conscious of it—according to predetermined patterns, which can often be traced back into prehistory.

Little has changed since Herodotus lived; basic comparisons of the present with past ages are manifold.[7] Perhaps this realization is a very recent one, dating from the time artists once again began to see loving, eating, being born, dying, sacrificing, sleeping, and dressing as processes basic to living. These old truths, now given new expression, shock us at first, but we have to realize that any attempt to describe human existence in our time must ask again: How do they bury their dead? How do they make sacrifices? How do they marry? These were the questions Herodotus asked about the Jews, the Egyptians, and other peoples he visited, and the answers characterized them. The same behavior patterns still interest us most—and characterize us best— today.

There may come a time when the art of the 1960s will be seen in its turn as an ethnological document, the product of an ethnology much broader than that of the 19th or 20th centuries, for the documents available for future study will show a much deeper insight into the constants of human development and an understanding of man as an inhabitant of this planet more penetrating than in the past. The factors that to Herodotus were so unambiguous that he could use them without a second thought to characterize the tribes he visited have lost so much of their universality during the millenniums needed for the development of Occidental civilization that today it is difficult to see the relationships between the cultural expressions of our time and the universal constants of human behavior.

The re-evaluation of the significance of the subconscious in the 20th century brought with it important discoveries. The meaning of the subconscious mind,

6   L. Levy-Bruhl. La mentalité primitive, Paris, 1922; E. Cassirer, Philosophie der symbo-
lischen Formen, 3 vols, Darmstadt, 1964.
7   Hermann Strasburger, ed., Herodot: Geschichten, Frankfurt-am-Main, 1961.

emphasized more and more as time passes, was summarized by Salvador Dali as early as 1934, in his writings on Surrealist art: "The subconscious has a symbolic language that is truly a universal language, for it does not depend on special habitude or state of culture or intelligence, but speaks with the vocabulary of the great vital content—sexual instinct, feeling of death, physical notion of the enigma of space—these vital constants are universally echoed in every human."

Even the most common and seemingly everyday action originates in the depths of the subconscious. And it is absolutely necessary for us to know this at a time when we are becoming accustomed to such aberrations as mass murder, mass imprisonment, and the physical, spiritual, and psychic regimentation and expropriation of people—to the point that "normal" demands for a new order of society expressed in terms of love, peace, flowers, children, freedom, and helping one's neighbor seem to us extravagant utopianism. Oscar Wilde realized that "A society is more corroded by the habitual imposition of sentences than by the occasional occurrence of crime." (1891)

Self-immolation as a political act, a photo of the dead Che Guevara, the political assassinations in America,[8] the student movements all over the world, men overcoming the earth's gravitational field to land on the moon, heart transplants and the implantation of artificial organs in the human body—all these things determine the climate of our spiritual situation and find their expression in paintings, sculpture, books, films, buildings, Happenings, and plays by contemporary artists.

Let us select one example from among many: the musical "Hair," by Jerome Ragni and James Rado, with music by Galt McDermott, a smash hit since its first performance in 1968 in the Biltmore Theater in New York. This production has made us newly conscious of the symbolic potential of hair: Hair as the expression of vitality, of resistance, of opposition, of independence, of power—of being human—combined with a simultaneous renewed reference to the ancient idea that the strength of a man lay in his hair.[9] How much can we really say about the unconscious, unspoken associations of this piece with the tribal rites (and the group performing "Hair" calls itself a tribe) that, in the past, used human hair and nails as magical charms? Indians collected the scalps of their fallen enemies, and hair plays an important role in Christian myth, not only in the story of Samson and Delila but also in the Christian concept of hell—hell is evil, carnal, and must be driven out of one's mind, repressed. Hair as a symbol recalls countless associations that are slowly finding their way into our consciousness again; the pop musical uses this symbol to ask the eternal questions about human existence: Where do I go? Why do I live? Why do I die?

8   Eduard Weinstein, "Symbolic Aspects of Presidential Assassination," Psychiatry, February, 1969.

9   Spencer Coxe, "The Great Hair Problem," Youth, June 18, 1967; Tom Wolfe, "The Hair Boys," in Pumphouse Gang, New York, 1968.

The point here, just as with the special accentuation of hair (primarily feminine, in this case) in the work of the Pre-Raphaelites, Lautréamont,[10] and Art Nouveau during the period when women were fighting for their emancipation on all fronts, is not one of eroticism alone; it concerns deep-seated problems of existence that require—even compel—visual expression. This is as true of the works of Burne-Jones, Rossetti, Beardsley, Klimt, and Khnopff as of the musical "Hair."

The primal symbol is continually re-expressed and reformulated, a process that brings with it continual re-evaluation. The same could be said of purification and expurgation rites, which can be traced from ancient Africa through Mesopotamia, Egypt, India, Japan, and the Christian world to their apotheosis in soap ads; of ceremonial forms of greeting and constants in the choice of partners and courtship; or of the rituals of eating, from the blood sacrifice to the saying of grace to today's table manners. All these taboos and rules of conduct have in common an interchange between play and reality; in all the forms invented by man throughout history to regulate personal and public behavior, one part equals the whole, "Pars pro toto."

New forms of living—new life styles—assert themselves within a frame of reference that remains, basically, constant. The patterns of behavior that have crystallized around developments in the arts since 1960 embody an irrationalism anchored in a definite system of values; this attitude has also taken root in the sciences,[11] the economy, advertising, politics, and other fields.[12] Communities have put new concepts of living into practice in the United States—in New York, California, Arizona, and Colorado—and in Europe—in London, Berlin, and Munich.[13] If they don't find an old villa, factory, or barn to live in, then they build their own housing, like the members of the commune in Libre, Colorado, who constructed their quarters using R. Buckminster Fuller's geodesic dome. Of course, the cost of aluminum and steel was prohibitive, so they used wood, plastic, or materials from the skeletons of abandoned cars, a plentiful source. Rolled steel paneling from the tops of old automobiles is a perfect material for a domed roof.

These practical attempts find their equivalents in the theories of young architects. Architecture und city planning are freeing themselves of inherited ideas. John M. Johansen said: "I am interested, then, in processes rather than finality, improvisation rather than predetermination, human imperfection rather than idealism, and the significant rather than the beautiful." Groups of architects like Archigram in London or the Metabolists in Tokyo[14] interpret architecture as a reality adapted to the living processes of society's

---

10 H. R. Lindner, "Lautréamont" (dissertation), Basel, 1947.
11 Karl Jaspers sees as characteristic of the new science its "open-ended" quality (Unfertigheit).
12 W. J. J. Gordon, Synectics, New York, 1961.
13 Prince Kropotkin gave an exact description of such communities, based on mutual help, in the 19th century. P. Heintz, Anarchismus und Gegenwart, Zurich, 1951.
14 Udo Kultermann, New Japanese Architecture (Rev. ed.), New York and London, 1967.   11

growth; Alison and Peter Smithson developed their "aesthetics of change";[15] P. Cook designed plug-in cities[16] and Ron Herron walking cities; Bourbonnais, Ruhnau, and Pinero have made suggestions for a mobile theater; Yona Friedmann is working out a general theory of mobility, and Konstantin Katavolos has developed a vision of architecture formed by chemical processes, architecture that happens—all in the 1960s.[17] However, the unexplored possibilities of self-built architecture have as get found no place in our static, entrenched, constructed environment (whose over-organized character could easily be changed fundamentally).

In many cases, communities of artists have come together to reinterpret and redesign their lives. Because their goal is total, all-encompassing, universal life, it is no wonder that these communities remind us of African compounds, North American Indian tribes, or Eskimo colonies in Greenland. Thus the function of the shaman, who gives these different primitive communities their center and direction, regains its significance in the 20th century.[18] The artist, if you will, is the shaman of modern society.

Alfred Lommel[19] has attempted to give a general definition of the meaning and function of the shaman. He emphasizes above all the importance of physical activity, the activation of the subconscious, and the fact that the shaman's work is always done in a trance; he is one step removed from the most important functions of the medicine man, the magician, or the sorcerer. The shaman does more. He holds his tribe—a group of people, a community —in balance. Lommel also points out the similarities between primitive and contemporary man: "The modern mass-man is much closer to the primitive group-man than the solitary individual was a few decades ago."

The shaman does not produce objects, although he is usually an artist in primitive communities, and he acts like an artist by renouncing the self and by bringing a sacrifice for society. In that he is himself engaged he activates healing forms of behavior in others. Seen in this light, the Happening is the consequence and expression of modern shamanism. Poets like Allan Ginsberg, William Burroughs, and Jean Genet, artists like Yves Klein, Manzoni, Oldenburg, and Beuys, composers like John Cage create through their personal presence. The result or effect of their engagement is never completely clear; the process itself is the important thing. The actions of the artist and those who cooperate with him—the community—are interrelated and change their character continually. The "madness" of the shaman—often misunderstood and written off with superficially applied clinical terminology—is the conditio, the only basis upon which a community of men can be returned to sanity.

15 Architect's Year Book 8, 1957.
16 Peter Cook, Architecture: Action and Plan, London, 1967.
17 Organics, 1960.
18 G. Nioradze, Der Schamanismus bei den sibirischen Völkern, Stuttgart, 1925; Mircea Eliade, Der Schamanismus, Zurich, 1947; Alfred Lommel, Shamanism, New York, 1967.
19 Lommel, Shamanism.

This ritual behavior, closer to prehistoric mystery cults than to so-called modern behavior, can be seen in all branches of art today.[20] Contemporary theater is strongly infused with it.[21] Irving Wardle wrote about the new theater in England and America: "They are both concerned with ritual. They aim in various ways to use the theater as an instrument of healing for a sick community; either through therapy or metaphysical ceremony."[22]

The members of the Living Theater, the La Mama Group and the Performance Group fulfill these functions, but only by challenging their own powers to the utmost, through complete human and artistic engagement. The fact that their activity is carried out in the heart of the community without the theatrical "props" that often isolate traditional theater from the audience (curtain, backdrop, prompter) indicates the high degree of aesthetic concentration they demand of themselves. Authenticity is becoming more and more important. Validity is no longer associated with the acted, the impersonated, and the manipulated, but with the truly experienced. This can and should be carried so far that the making of a film, a painting, or a Happening changes the life of its maker. Creation as a process, the result of which has traditionally been called art, is capable of affecting and altering life itself.

The German artist Joseph Beuys has been directly compared with a shaman. When he goes into action, he looks "much more the zealous shaman than the clown. Engaged to the point of exhaustion, he transforms absurd theater into 'existential pantomime.'" This is a most apt identification of the processes of contemporary art with the behavior of the shaman. Beuys himself was one of the first to grasp the political relevance of his action: he founded a political party.

An objective analysis of the events and processes which determine the nature of contemporary art leads to the conclusion that the unique rhythms of life and nature are again playing an important role. Mutual respect and trust are once more expected to be the bases of community life. In disagreement with conventional wisdom on the subject, Max Born, one of the greatest natural scientists of the 20th century, concluded that "... in human society, technology and war are incompatible," and gave one of the first progressive and humane definitions of technology. Love has become the key word, just as it always had been in ancient Africa, in Greenland, in Asia, and in the North America of the Indians.

Nature and art are no longer opposites in the minds of many artists. Dean Fleming uses nature in his sculptures and structures as a role-playing element—the different manifestations of trees in spring, summer, autumn, and winter are an integral part of the total aesthetic effect—and Dennis Oppen-

20   A. Horneffer, Symbolik der Mysterien-Gründe, Heidelberg, 1924; E. E. Kellett, The Story of Myths, New York, 1927; L. A. Govinde, Mandala, Der Heilige Kreis, Zurich, 1961.
21   R. J. Lee, "Irony and Religious Mystery in the Contemporary Theater," Soundings, Fall, 1969.
22   Irving Wardle, "Transatlantic Ritual," Yale Theater, No. 2, 1968.

heim thinks of natural growth and the effects of farming on the land as aesthetic processes. Richard Long gives nature definite modulations, and he includes moving people and their changing frames of reference (and his own) in his conceptions. Giuseppe Penone ties trees together and influences their growth. Barry Flanagan alters the surface of the sea, and Robert Morris changes the climate of an entire region. Peter Hutchinson looks on processes of decay as they develop in huge glass tubes on the floor of the ocean or in various climates as artistic phenomena. The beauty in such processes has been newly discovered by contemporary artists.

The art of the past few years shows that, again, the artist cannot afford to overlook technological developments. The shaman of our time differs in this respect from his counterpart among, say, the natives of the Siberian tundra. He knows and has mastered modern technology. He knows and has mastered the mass media so crucial to our urban lives. He is searching for new areas of freedom within these media.

Technological development during the 1960s has brought with it the relatively non–value-oriented information of the mass media, which has resulted in freedom to an extent unknown even to the previous generation. "Many doors are now open (they open according to where we give our attention). Once through, looking back, no walls or doors are seen," said John Cage.[23] Television is part and parcel of our daily life; thus culture and society are no longer separate in principle, as they still are in "modern art." Museums, theaters, concert halls, etc., are cultural institutions set apart from daily life, while television is part of almost everybody's immediate environment. So divisions between life and art disappear, and the idea that television has nothing to do with art is a great help in this respect: "One advantage for television artists is that their audience does not look upon television as 'art.'"[24]

During the 1950s, in spite of all advances made in technology, narrow, personally defined knowledge and fixed content in art remained basic values. Since then, television has become so ubiquitous and influential that "television culture" has replaced culture in the traditional sense. The new culture is commercial; it controls technology and is ruled by it at the same time, even though television is still used like the film medium (just as the first automobiles looked very much like carriages). Television culture has been seen in an almost completely negative light since its inception; it offers hardly any peaks to take it out of the realm of daily life. The painting, the symphony, and the monument are the expressions of an activity characterized by individualism, and they communicate exclusivity. In contrast, the hallmarks of our era are mass production, apathy, mass consumption, and the eventual goal of mass creativity. A new "humanism" is showing its head, a new and, paradoxically, individual responsibility, and a new belief in the importance of life itself

23 John Cage, A Year from Monday, Middleton, Conn., 1967, p. 165.
24 John S. Margolies in Art in America, September–October, 1969, p. 50.

above all the abstractions that dominated the artistic conscience over the past centuries.

The mass consumption of art—and we should consider television, in addition to other manifestations of intermedia, as the art form of our time—destroys the inherited and ancient values formulated by an elite culture that ignored the masses. The concept of quality itself must be redefined and adapted to contemporary society. It is even conceivable that the word quantity is already of much greater significance.

1

4

20

6

8

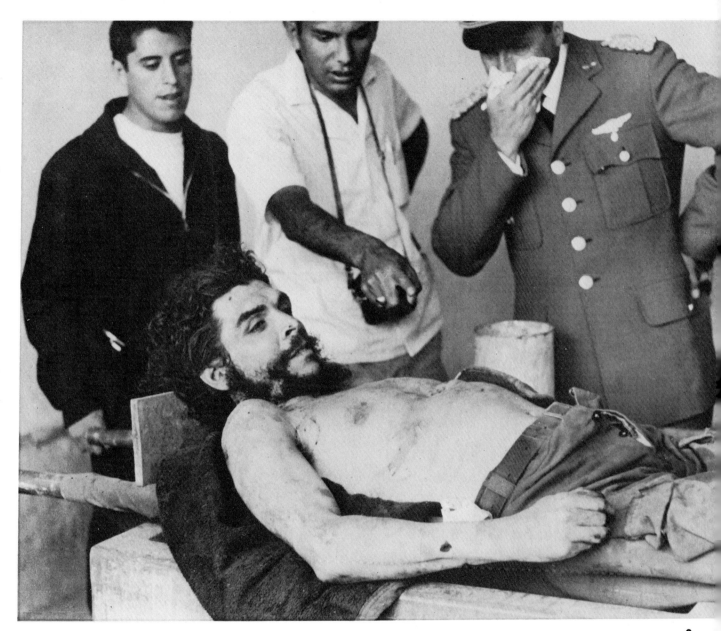

12

16

"If we persist in our restless desire to know everything about the universe and ourselves, then we must not be afraid of what the artist brings back from his voyage of discovery."

Herbert Read

Among the spiritual ancestors of the elements that, taken together, are called intermedia (and of the general intellectual atmosphere of the mid-20th century) are such men as the Marquis de Sade,[25] the Comte de Lautréamont, Rimbaud, Mallarmé, Jarry, Scheerbart, Yeats, Maeterlinck, Apollinaire, and many others who have yet to be integrated into the hardened categories of formal art history. The traditions go back much further, and they are not limited to Europe. African dance, for example, should be seen as a ritual uniting the community through music, movement, rhythm, literature, painting, and many other components. Mircea Eliade reports that the Uitoto cannibals say: "We only work so that we can dance,"[26] an attitude quite similar to the outlook on life held by many in the second half of the 20th century.

Japanese Zen Buddhism has also contributed to new forms of meditation in our culture, which has in addition adopted such diverse models as the ritual of the Catholic Mass and the tradition of Indian music. The antithesis of Catholic ritual, the Black Mass, has also been drawn upon, enriched with the philisophy of the alchemists and with forms taken from ancient Jewish ritual.[27]

It is characteristic of these phenomena that they cannot be explained within the historical development of any one medium, that different threads come together in each case, and that it is precisely their mutual influence and en-

25   M. Heine, Le Marquis de Sade et le roman noir, Paris, 1933; G. Gorer, The Revolutionary Ideas of the Marquis de Sade, London, 1934.
26   S. Preuss, Religion und Mythologie der Uitoto, Göttingen, 1921.
27   H.T.F. Rhodes, The Satanic Mass, London, 1954; G. Zacharias, Satanskult und Schwarze Messe, Wiesbaden, 1964.

richment, crossing all boundaries, that is the common bond between them. The "commedia dell' arte" used significant elements of this kind—improvisation, audience participation, ironic portraits, and a wide range of informal representation. These are also features of countless folk plays, which have gone largely unnoticed by historians.

Lautréamont, who expressed such thoughts as "poetry must be created by all, not by one"[28] in his "Poésies," pushed his poetry to the frontiers of feeling and thus became the most important link between the Marquis de Sade and the 20th century. His unique combination of controlled thought and freed fantasy is well captured in one of his programmatic formulations: "We live in a time too eccentric for us to wonder, even for a moment, about what could happen."[29]

Lautréamont uses evil to force the reader's emotional hand: he demands that we take sides. His letters tell us that the rape, sacrifice, sodomy, homosexuality, crime, and greed described in minute detail in his "Maldoror" were meant to provoke his audience into action. To describe the world, including the realms of the imagination, he created antitypes and anti-images. During the late 19th century other important forms of intermedia were developed in various fields, notably in the plays of Alfred Jarry and Maurice Maeterlinck, in the theater of Constantin Stanislavsky, and in the early films of Georges Méliés. And the composer Alexander Scriabin fused music, space, color, and movement into a ritualistic whole in his "Prometheus," thus reaching a cultish plateau at one remove from the total work of art for which Richard Wagner had striven during the heady period marked by the founding of the German nation.

Wagner had, in his own way, already combined the different disciplines of literature, music, and theater in his works, but artistic experiments during the last decade of the 19th century Sar surpassed his conceptions. Paul Scheerbart not only gave the imagination access to a cosmos of new realities in his novels, but also sketched situations for the theater that foreshadowed the activities of the Dadaists in his revolutionary writings. Even the poem consisting entirely of sounds, a form uniting literature and music and still thought by most to be a Dadaist invention, was fully realized by Scheerbart in his novel "Ich liebe Dich" (1897). Above all, Scheerbart had close connections with artists and architects who kept him up to date on the developments in other branches of art; an outgrowth of this was his formative influence on the glass architecture of Expressionism.[30] The cross-breeding of different areas of art was considerably advanced by his catholic interest and unbounded fantasy.

28 Lautréamont, Gesamtwerk, Heidelberg, 1954, p. 321. G. Bachelard, Lautréamont, Paris, 1938; M. Blanchot, Lautréamont et Sade, Paris, 1949.

29 Lautréamont, Gesamtwerk, p. 263.

30 Udo Kultermann, "Paul Scheerbart und die Architektur des 20. Jahrhunderts," in Handbuch des Bauwesens, Stuttgart, 1962.

Expressionism and Futurism were primary pre-Dada impulses. Both these movements, mainly German and Italian in origin, gathered impetus in the decade before World War I. Expressionism was basically a literary movement, pervading theater and films as well as poems and novels. Expressionist thinking was based on Nietzsche's re-evaluation of the Dionysian sensibility;[31] he redirected men's eyes to the culture of ancient Greece. An early example of Expressionist thought is Oskar Kokoschka's drama "Mörder, Hoffnung der Frauen" ("Murderers, Hope of Women"), written in 1910, which already contains significant elements of the reformation of bourgeois theater later attempted in Germany.

Film was the key art form in which all streams of pre-war thought converged. Theater, photography, acting, literature, architecture, and sculpture all found their place in this new, total medium. "The Cabinet of Dr. Caligari" (1920) by Rudolf Wiener, designed by Hermann Warm, unfolded against a backdrop of Expressionist film architecture. Hans Poelzig, in addition to his great architectural achievements, among them many movie theaters, also designed stage sets. In the sets for the film "Der Golem," after the novel by Gustav Meyrinck, he captured in an Expressionist idiom the atmosphere of old Prague, a city that stimulated an entire generation of Expressionist poets. And the figuration of Hermann Finsterlin's architectural work—outsized men and women designed to be lived in, even buildings in the form of couples making love—are fascinating embodiments of the Expressionist vision.

The roots of Futurism, also basically a literary movement, are likewise pre-World War I.[32] Anton Biulio Bragaglia demonstrated in his "Fotodinamismo," published in Rome in 1911, new approaches to visual design. In 1913 Russolo worked out Brutismo, which might be called the art of noise. The first performances in this genre took place in 1914 in London and Milan. Noises from daily life were used as elements of acoustic composition. In this way, the artist created a new relationship between himself and reality. The organizer of the Futurists, Marinetti, found in his poetry new connections between art and reality through his attempts to free words from their traditional connotations and use them for their sensual values.

The Dadaist movement introduced a new phase in art in that it brought art and life closer together than ever before. The experience of World War I and the intellectual ferment that resulted from artists living in strange surroundings as emigrants generated new philosophies and forms of expression—exemplified by the Cabaret Voltaire in Zurich or the 291 Gallery in New York, mutual influence of artists and media became a fact of life. Above all, Dada redefined the social function of art. Art and propaganda were united, a relationship introduced early by Kurt Hiller in Berlin in his "neopathetic cabaret" (1910) and his Cabaret Gnu (1911).

31 D. Sharp, Modern Architecture and Expressionism, London, 1966.
32 J. C. Taylor, Futurism, New York, 1961.

All these efforts culminated in 1916, when the Cabaret Voltaire was founded in Zurich.[33] Here, finally, was an institution, founded on the initiative of Hugo Ball, working together with Tristan Tzara, Hans Arp, Richard Hülsenbeck, and many others, that raised poetry and music, theater, dance, and the visual arts to a new plane, divesting them of their content–oriented significance and unchaining them from Meaning.

The sound poem was polished and purified during this time; simultaneity of poetry and music was propagated, collage and photomontage were invented, chance and improvisation were given a place in the arts of theater and the dance, and even sensationalism became part of the Dadaists' all-encompassing activity. As early as 1916, Jacques Vaché caused a series of scandals by submitting deliberately falsified "factual" reports to the newspapers. This certainly created a new relationship between the artist and his public—and simultaneously unmasked the insanity of war.

The same years saw Duchamp and Picabia in Alfred Stieglitz's 291 Gallery in New York, Johannes Baader in Berlin, Max Ernst in Cologne, and many others in other places confronting the realities of bourgeois life. A key figure here is the boxer Arthur Craven; his ingenious actions invariably caused an uproar. On April 23, 1916, for instance, he challenged the heavyweight champion of the world, Jack Johnson, to a fight in Madrid, and was knocked cold in the first round. An another occaision, before an audience of invited ladies waiting to hear his lecture, he disrobed completely and let himself be led away by the police. He never gave up the attempt to replace art with life itself. He wanted to give life form—Gestalt—and to articulate it anew. Life, for him, was an aesthetic adventure.

This attitude would have been unthinkable without Dadaism. A similar philosophy found expression in Marcel Duchamp's new conception of art.[34] As early as 1913 Duchamp mounted a bicycle wheel on a kitchen stool as an epigram on movement. He wanted to make pure reality cogent by changing it, by putting it into new contexts.

Thus developed the concept of the "ready-made," in which were embodied the arbitrariness of the accidental as well as an openness to play and association. In 1915 Duchamp bought a snow shovel, which he exhibited with the title "In Advance of a Broken Arm". During the next few years, Duchamp applied this conception in other fields of art. His work in ballet, film, literature, sculpture, and painting, in both Surrealist and kinetic art, is so diverse as to be almost impossible to catalogue. From his actions and his ideas, from his kind of conceptual art, Duchamp's influence has spread to many streams of 20th century art.

Another important progenitor of intermedia was Kurt Schwitters, an artist

33   Udo Kultermann, "Café Voltaire," Augenblick, 2, No. 3, 1956; M. Prosenc, Die Dadaisten in Zürich, Bonn, 1967.
34   R. Lebel, Marcel Duchamp, Paris, 1959; Cologne, 1962.

who was laughed at by most of his contemporaries.[35] He was involved in almost every medium, from architecture to sculpture and painting, and from music and poetry to advertising and even environmental design. His attempts at integration on the basis of a new relationship of the artist to reality—expressed programmatically by the word merz, picked at random from his visual environment—led to new meanings and contents. Both merz theater and merz poetry are historically important predecessors of current developments in art.

In 1921 Schwitters wrote in the magazine "Der Ararat": "Take a dentist's drill, a meat grinder, the cowcatcher from a streetcar, buses and automobiles, bicycles, tandems and their tires, also war tires of synthetic rubber, and deform them. Take lights and deform them in the most brutal manner imaginable. Have locomotives crash into each other, take curtains and porters, let spider webs dance with window ledges and smash sniveling glass. Heat steam boilers till they explode to produce billows of railway smoke. Take petticoats and other similar things like shoes and fake hair, ice skates too, and throw them in the right place, just where they belong, and always at the right time. If you feel like it, take foot angles too, and self-shooters, hell machines, the tin fish and the funnel, everything in artistically deformed condition, of course. Hoses are especially recommended. In short, take everything from a genteel lady's hairnet to an imperialist's screw, all of the proper size and scale, according to the demands of the work. Even people can be used. People can be tied to stage flats. People can even take an active part, they can even appear in their daily situation, speak two-leggedly, even in sensible sentences. Now, begin to munch and marry all the materials together."

Schwitters anticipated the totality of current visual and conceptual experience: he joined music and literature; architecture, sculpture and painting lost their exclusive identities in his "merz" constructions; and through a combination of the propaganda campaigns he and Theo van Doesburg led through provincial German and Dutch towns and his advertising methods and public provocations, he opened new stretches of aesthetic land for the settlers to follow. Hans Richter wrote about him: "And so he pasted, nailed, poetasted, set type, hawked, printed, composed, collaged, declaimed, whistled, clinched and loved, roaring, without regard for anyone, for the public, for any technique whatsoever, for traditional art, or for himself. He did everything and did most of it simultaneously. The goal he had in mind was not so much the total work of art in the sense that Ball or even Kandinsky meant it—a synchronous combination of all the arts—but rather an unceasing obliteration of all borders between the arts and their integration into one, including the machine as "an abstraction of the human mind," including kitsch, chair legs, singing, and shuddering. In reality, HE, Kurt Schwitters, was the total work of art."[36]

35 W. Schmalenbach, Kurt Schwitters, Cologne, 1967; Kate Steinetz, Kurt Schwitters, Berkeley, Calif., 1968.
36 Hans Richter. Dada: Art and Anti-Art, New York, 1965.

In addition to Germany, Switzerland, and America, Soviet Russia played an important role in formulating the new definition of the relationship between art and reality; its contribution was influenced strongly by Russian artists' search for social responsibility.[37] Even before the Revolution, new movements occured in the theater (Stanislavsky), in ballet (Diaghilev), and in music (Scriabin), which helped lay the foundations for the new conceptions of art that crystalized around 1917. Decisive work was done by Kasimir Malevitch, El Lissitzky, Rodchenko, and Vladimir Tatlin in the visual arts, by Leonidov and the Wesnin brothers and Mielnikov in architecture, by Eisenstein, Pudovkin, and Vertov in film, and by Mayakovsky in literature.

Their attempts were unified by a shared desire to build a new state on a new cultural foundation. Vladimir Tatlin's program for the Constructivist group was probably the most radical and forward-looking of all. To quote from it:

1. Down with art, long live technology.
2. Religion is a lie. Art is a lie.
3. Destroy the last ties of human thought with art.
4. Down with the cultivation of artistic traditions. Long live the constructivist technicians.
5. Down with the kind of art that obscures human incapacity.
6. The collective art of the present is constructive life (1920).[38]

This manifesto was one of the first expressions of the new, "collective" life, a life understood to be creative. Similar ideas were current in Holland at the same time. Piet Mondrian also predicted a situation in which the artist would no longer be necessary: everyone would live in a completely constructed milieu, which would preclude the need for art because it would be so perfectly and harmoniously designed. The metaphorical aspect of art—long one of its basic "givens"—was here avoided: metaphor was replaced by the transformation of materials and content; for Tatlin, that which is made was the same as that which is meant. He worked within an existing situation, without intellectual or figurative references. This is a conception of art relevant to the new society of the 20th century, but a conception that had to wait until the 1960s to be carried on consequentially.

Environmental design, first couched in terms of art, carried over naturally into architecture and city planning. Tatlin and other artists involved themselves directly in the processes of production and conceived architectural projects that are extremely significant for the history of architecture in the 20th century. The tower that Tatlin designed for the 1920 Third International in Moscow, for example, included movable rooms hung in a huge spiral framework. El Lissitzky's "cloud hangers" are epoch-making designs for a new synthesis of architecture and city planning and are much more daring than much of the work being done in this field today.

Russia was the center of creative development in other areas as well. The

37   Camilla Gray, The Great Experiment, New York and London, 1962.
38   Naum Gabo, Gabo, Neuchâtel, 1960, p. 156.

film, above all else, went through a revolutionary phase, laying the ground-work for decades to come. Eisenstein, Pudovkin, Vertov,[39] and others who came to film from the theater, or, like Vertov, from photo reporting, reached plateaus of creativity in film that are true jumping off points for the inter-media of the 1960s. Eisenstein not only made use of the montage in his aggressive film work, he also staged theater outside the walls of the theater: "Gas Masks" (1923–24) was performed on site in a gas factory.

Throughout the rest of Europe during the 1920s, such men as Pirandello in Italy, Brecht in Germany, and Artaud in France worked on new forms of theater. Common to all three was the desire for greater authenticity, the expansion of the physical scene, the integration of musical, film, and dance elements into the stage performance—thought by all three playwrights to be too narrowly defined traditionally—and the participation of the audience. Oskar Schlemmer developed an even more far-reaching conception for the Bauhaus stage: he also unified dance, space, sculpture, painting, and movement into a new whole. He attempted to expand his means of expression in order to maximize the artist's opportunities for effective creation.[40]

The actor, poet, and playwright Antonin Artaud very possibly had a direct effect on the American Happening. His work "The Theater and its Double"[41] appeared for the first time in English in 1958. Artaud's attempts to unify different areas of art in the theater began in the 1930s. He wrote: "As soon as the theater is aware of this language in the room, i.e., the language of noises, cries, lights, of sound painting, it must compose it into hieroglyphics of reality. It must make use of its symbolic contents and the various connections with all matter on all planes with the help of persons and things."[42]

Dance should be mentioned here: it was given a new basis by Isadora Duncan, Loie Fuller, Ruth St. Denis, and Nijinsky. The work of Mary Wigman and Martha Graham built on this foundation, and those who learned from them (Alwin Nikolais, Merce Cunningham, Paul Taylor, Marilyn Wood) transformed much of European and American dance.[43]

Another root of the intermedia lies in film. The pioneer work of Méliès and Griffith, Dreyer and Murnau, Eisenstein and Pudovkin in this medium brought together and united many previously disparate disciplines: theater and music, acting, acrobatics and pantomime, painting, sculpture and architecture—all raised to a higher power by the incomparable possibilities inherent in the film technique.[44] Filmmakers like Eggeling and Richter also created new

39 N. P. Abramov, Dziga Vertov, Lyon, 1965.
40 O. Schlemmer, Die Bühne im Bauhaus, Munich, 1925; O. Schlemmer, L. Moholy-Nagy, and F. Molnar, The Theater of the Bauhaus, Middleton, Conn., 1961; O. Schlemmer, Der Mensch, Mainz, 1969.
41 Antonin Artaud, The Theater and Its Double, New York, 1958.
42 J. Hort, Antonin Artaud: The Suicide of Society, Geneva, 1960.
43 Walter Sorell, The Dance Through the Ages, New York, 1967.
44 B. Balazac, Theory of the Film, London, 1952; S. Kracauer, Theory of Film, New York, 1961.

frames of reference with their experimental work. Dali and Bunuel's collaboration was significant.[45] Joseph Cornell opened up dimensions in his films, which were not fully understood until the 1960s. Stan Brackhage, who worked with Cornell initially, was stimulated by his approach. Comedies and cartoons are also recognized as important sources for the art of the 1960s. Charlie Chaplin, Buster Keaton, Walt Disney's animated cartoons, and the Marx brothers completely redefined the relationship between art and the audience because they reached masses of people and moved them. Film as mass medium became the crucial discipline of the new art. Stan Brackhage acknowledged the reason: "The movies were my religion as a child and still are, to all of the child in me. The attraction was/is, thus, the need for ritual."

The Surrealist movement is another important source of the new desire for unity in the arts which arose in the 1960s.[46] Founded in 1924 by André Breton, together with a splinter group from the Dadaists around Tristan Tzara, the members of the Surrealist movement did not limit themselves to art; they were passionately interested in all areas of modern life, from psychoanalysis to politics—in short, in modern reality.

The Surrealist movement was christened and launched in 1924 with the premiere of Erik Satie's ballet "Relâche." Satie's music had shocked the public from the beginning (he began composing shortly before the turn of the century), and titles like "Dances to Run Away From," "Pieces in the Shape of a Pear," and "Three Limp Preludes for a Dog" served to incense his audiences the more. He utilized reality and its conditions in his work, too. In "Parade" (1917), he used the sounds of typewriters, factory sirens, and combustion engines as elements of musical composition. But a unique chance to realize his wildest ideas came through the cooperation of Marcel Duchamp, Man Ray, and Francis Picabia. In the first act of "Relâche" (literally, "no show") spotlights were directed into the audience so that, dazzled, they could hardly make out what was happening on stage: a fireman chainsmoked cigarettes and poured water continuously from one bucket into another. Marcel Duchamp, naked, played Adam to an equally undressed model's Eve, after the painting by Lucas Cranach. Man Ray, who sat impassively near the curtain during the performance, stood up at regular intervals and measured the dimensions of the stage. During intermission a film by a young cameraman was shown: "Entr'acte" by René Clair, after a sketch of Francis Picabia. This movie, with its burial in Luna Park and showing Marcel Duchamp playing chess with Man Ray on the roof of the Théâtre des Champs Elysées while Erik Satie kibitzed, is one of the most important documents of film history. In the second act of "Relâche" Jean Borlin danced; the climax was assured when Satie and Picabia drove into the theater in a 5–HP Citroen to greet the howling, angry audience. The

45 T. Mussman, "The Surrealist Film", Artforum, September, 1966.
46 M. Nadeau, Histoire du Surréalisme, Paris, 1945; D. Wyss, Der Surrealismus, Heidelberg, 1950; Marcel Jean, Geschichte des Surrealismus, Cologne, 1961.

introduction to the program contains the following words: "Relâche is life, life like I love it: Completely of today, not yesterday and not tomorrow."[47] All the events staged by Dadaists in New York, Paris, and other cities were dedicated to bridging the gap between art and life. They wanted to articulate life directly, to be a part of it, to have a direct effect on the political realities of the day. Demonstration was their forte. And internal, primarily political, differences soon divided the Dadaists, as they do all movements; dadaism was a movement, a movement whose interests knew no traditional, categorical bounds.

A key figure here is Salvador Dali.[48] Occasionally working with Max Ernst or Marcel Duchamp, he came up with a number of significant ideas that can be considered seminal to the Happenings and events of the 1960s. Dali visited Sigmund Freud shortly before the scientist died; like Freud, but using aesthetic means, Dali devoted his life work to the exploration of the subconscious. Surrealist film was the joint product of Dali and Luis Bunuel, indeed, their "L'Age d'or" was something like a Surrealist community project: Dali and Bunuel produced it; Ernst, Aragon, Breton, Char, Crevel, Dali, Eluard, Péret, Tzara, and many others played in it. The film raised public provocation to the status of a method. The righteous indignation of the audience was answered by the publication of a flyer entitled "Christian Illiteracy." The film was banned.

Later, Dali made himself unwelcome with the Surrealists themselves by denigrating Lenin, and, according to Marcel Jean, he wasn't beyond showing an uncomfortable interest in Hitler and National Socialism. In 1934 Dali was given a mock trial by the Surrealists, in which the villian played himself. In the end, however, Dali's paranoiac methods proved more penetrating than most of the more doctrinaire members of the movement liked to admit. The numerous events he staged, rather like Happenings in character, were always designed to transform reality, including the brutal political situation of the 1930s, so as to reveal its deeper meaning. The essence of Dali's method is magic, despite the fact that the public considers him a charlatan. His intelligence and an extensive knowledge of history, which often allows him to see things in perspective, fed his urge to put life in all its aspects in the spotlight. This is a form of modern shamanism, using wit, jokes, comedy, and absurdity to strike deeper into the collective consciousness of our era.

Various tendencies of Constructivism, Surrealism, and other movements converge in the work of John Cage. Zen Buddhism and Indian philosophy also influenced him; the primary source of his music remains, however, the modern tradition, especially as represented by Arnold Schoenberg. Cage's use of chance comes perhaps from Dada. The uniqueness of his music—and his personality—has influenced almost all areas of contemporary culture.

47 Picabia quoted in Marcel Jean, Geschichte des Surrealismus, Cologne, 1961, p. 91.
48 Salvador Dali, The Secret Life of Salvador Dali, New York, 1968.

In painting, Jackson Pollock introduced real physical involvement—what might be called a subjective eruption of action or even the unification of painting and dance. Georges Mathieu celebrated the act of painting before his audiences, changing costumes as he went. Piero Manzoni carried similar principles even further with his concept of an endless line leading beyond the boundaries of human space, and Fontana approached his sliced canvases in the same manner. The members of the Gutai group also work along similar lines. Cutting flat planes, breaking through walls, and expanding closed spaces have all won new iconographic meaning.[49]

Artists want not merely to blur the boundary lines between individual disciplines, they want to tear those boundaries down. Nothing stands in their way. Anything from any area of art that can be combined with something else from another area is combined, by force if necessary, obliterating some distinations between art and life that existed as recently as 1960. Yves Klein used girls as "living paintbrushes"; Manzoni signed nude models and declared his artist friends to be officially certificated works of art; Otto Mühl and Günter Brus recommended an exhibition of people as the Austrian contribution to the Venice Biennale in 1968: "Human objects from old people's homes in Vienna sit on pedestals—name, age, illnesses, blows fate has dealt them, identifying marks, and skills all inscribed on a brass plate." "Living sculptures" were exhibited by Pi Lind in Stockholm in 1969; Peter Kuttner, Stuart Brisley, and Janet Deuters presented themselves on September 28, 1969, in a cage in the Chessington Zoo in Surrey as examples of Homo sapiens, and in 1969 Andy Warhol rented the members of his group to a paying public. The history of Happenings and the intermedia has yet to be written. The beginnings go back to the 1950s.[50] John Cage staged Happenings early in that decade, and the Gutai group in Osaka worked from 1955 to 1959.[51] Allan Kaprow's first untitled Happening took place in 1958; Yves Klein exhibited his "white room" in Paris, and Hundertwasser wrote his "Mould Manifesto Against Rationalism in Architecture" in the same year. In October, 1959, "18 Happenings in 6 Parts," by Allan Kaprow, took place in the Reuben Gallery in New York, Nam June Paik celebrated his "Hommage à John Cage" in the Galerie 22 in Düsseldorf, and Jean Tinguely exhibited his drawing machine in the First Biennale des Jeunes in Paris. In December of the same year Hundertwasser and Brock painted an endless line in the Hochschule für bildende Künste in Hamburg, and Red Grooms staged another early New York Happening, "The Burning Building."

49 For example, Jim Dine's "The Smiling Workman" (1960); Saburo Murakami's "Running Through" (1962); F. Tiziano's "Destruction of a Poem," Finmàlbo (1967).
50 Michael Kirby, Happenings, New York, 1965; Udo Kultermann, "Pop und Hap, die realisierte Dynamik in der zeitgenössischen Kunst," Artis, 3, 1965; J-J. Lebel, Le Happening, Paris, 1966, O. Massotta et al, Happening, Buenos Aires, 1967; Allan Kaprow, Assemblage, Environments, and Happenings, New York, 1967.
51 Udo Kultermann, "Happenings Wiege stand in Osaka," Artis, January, 1966; M. Cohen, "Japan's Gutai Group," Art in America, November–December, 1968.

1960 was the decisive year. Robert Whitman made "The Small Cannon," Allan Kaprow "The Big Laugh," and Red Grooms "The Magic Train Ride" (all in the Reuben Gallery, New York). Then came "The Smiling Workman" by Jim Dine, "Snapshots from City" by Claes Oldenburg, "A Small Smell" by Robert Whitman, and Allan Kaprow's "Coca-Cola, Shirley Cannonball?" In March of 1960, Jean Tinguely watched as his "Hommage à New York" destroyed itself in the garden of the Museum of Modern Art. Jean-Jacques Lebel held a "Cérémonie Funèbre" in Venice, and Yves Klein introduced the "anthropometries" of his blue period to the public. In the fall of 1960 the Reuben Gallery hosted another series of Happenings—"The Car Crash" by Jim Dine, "American Moon" by Robert Whitman, and "The Shining Bed," also by Dine. "Iron-works-Fotodeath" by Oldenburg and "A Spring Happening" by Kaprow took place in February and March of that year, respectively, also in the Reuben Gallery.

On October 16, 1961, Karlheinz Stockhausen, together with Nam June Paik, Hans G. Helms, Mary Bauermeister, and many other artists, presented his "Originale" in Cologne for the first time. In 1962 came "Injun" by Claes Oldenburg and "A Service for the Dead" and "Words" by Kaprow (March). Jean-Jacques Lebel presented "Pour Conjurer l'Esprit de Catastrophe" in the Galerie Cordier Paris. The year 1962 also saw performances of many Fluxus Happenings in various German and Dutch cities. Members of the Fluxus group included Joseph Beuys, George Maciunas, George Brecht, Nam June Paik, La Monte Young, Dick Higgins, Knowles, Koepke, Patterson, Robert Filliou, Vostell, and Williams. Happenings in Paris were greatly influenced by Tetsumi Kudo, who performed his "Philosophy of Impotence" in 1962 and "Harakiri of Humanism" at the Musée d'Art Moderne in 1963.

In 1963 the Happenings of Otto Mühl and Hermann Nitsch brought the scene to Vienna. In March of the same year a Festival of Happenings was held on George Segal's farm, in which Kaprow, Dick Higgins, La Monte Young, Yvonne Rainer, Wolf Vostell, and others took part. In July Kaprow staged a Happening in the Paris department store Au Bon Marché and another ("Out") in December at the International Writers Conference in Edinburgh. In 1964 Kaprow did his "Birds" in Carbondale, Illinois, "Orange" in Miami, "Paper" at the University of California in Berkeley, and "Household" at Cornell University in Ithaca, New York. On the twentieth anniversary of the murder of the men who tried to assassinate Hitler, an action entitled "June 20th, 1964" took place in Germany, organized by Beuys, Brock, Filliou, Koepke, and others. It led to a direct confrontation with the students. Happenings also took place in Finland, Spain, Holland, England, Czechoslovakia, Hungary, and Poland in 1964. Milan Knizak carried out his "Individual Demonstration," Gabor Altorjay worked in Budapest and Edward Krasinski in Warsaw. In October 1967 the Russian group Dvizdjenje staged a Happening in Leningrad with the title "1917," in which film, music, literature, the visual arts, and the nearest Lenin monument were included.

In the years following there were numerous Happenings in New York, Paris, 43

Vienna, Düsseldorf, Buenos Aires, Tokyo, and London. Undaunted by the many reports that the Happening had died, activity in this, the key area of the intermedia, continued to grow. We should realize that significant changes in form have taken place, although they may not yet be included in the category of Happenings.

An important new stage was reached by the "Nine Evenings of Theater and Engineering," which took place in 1966 in the Armory on 25th Street in New York. Engineers teamed up with artists to create the show, a marriage of art and technology. Such different artists as John Cage, Lucinda Childs, Oyvind Fahlström, Deborah Hay, Robert Rauschenberg, Yvonne Rainer, Robert Whitman, and David Tudor worked together with engineers to put together the completely programmed performance. It put the intermedia on a new plane of sophistication and opened up many new perspectives.

17

18

19

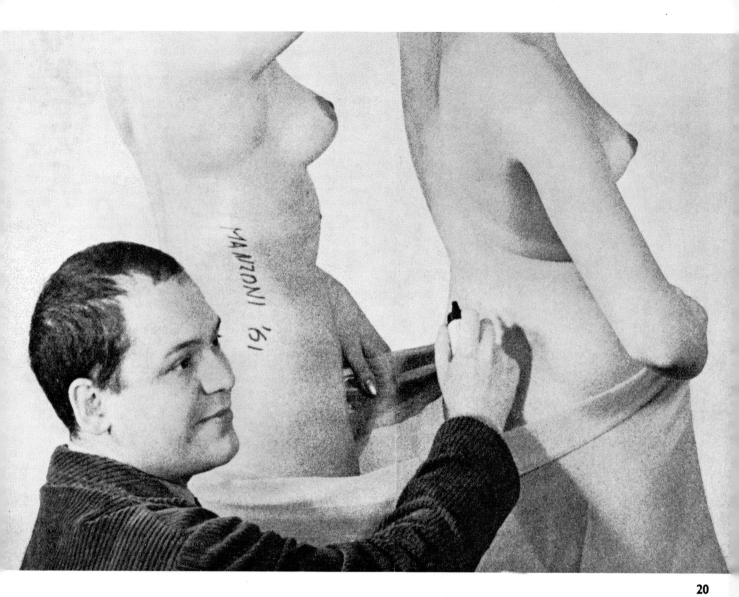

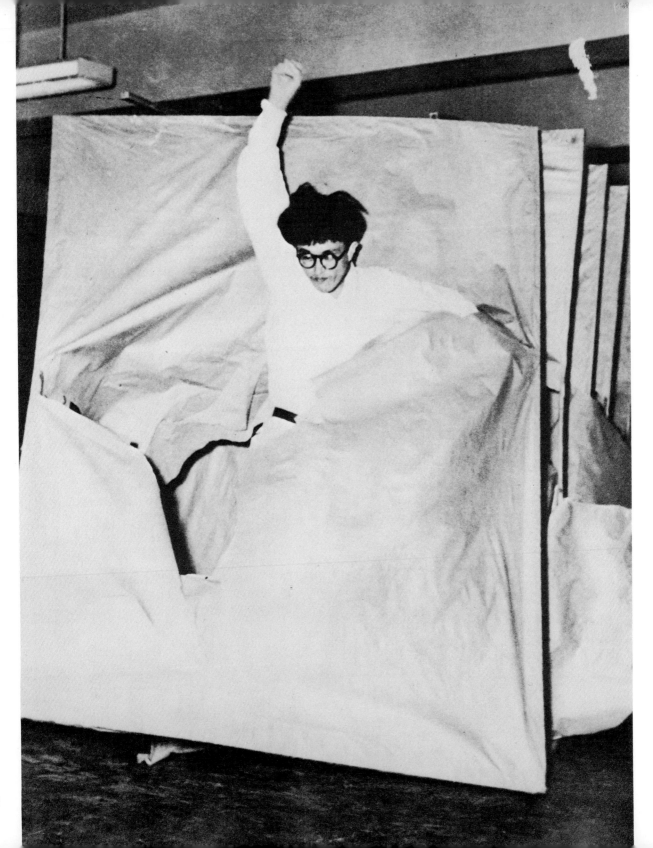

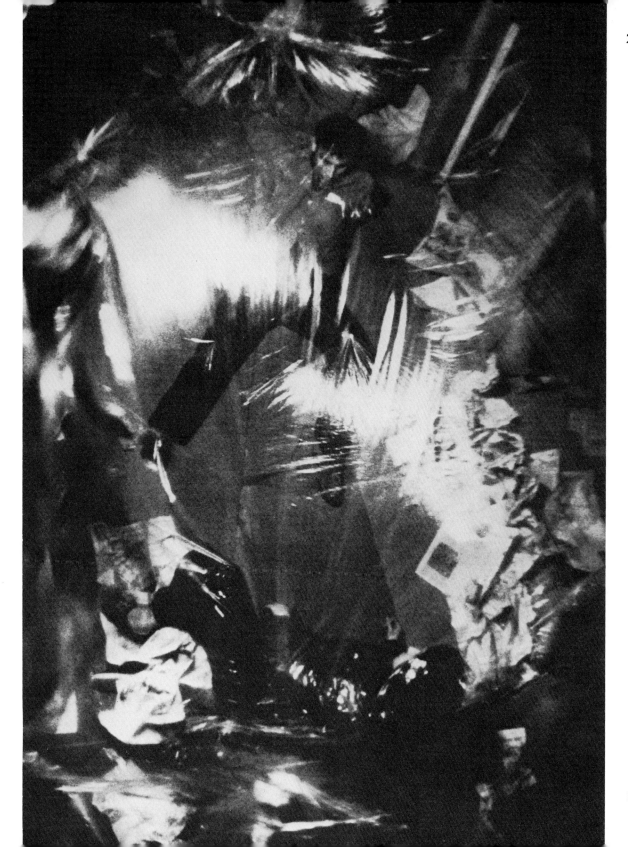

ANTI - PROCES

« Il faut abolir l'idée de jugement »
Marcel DUCHAMP.

Manifestation collective

organisée par

ALAIN JOUFFROY et JEAN-JACQUES LEBEL

DU 29 AVRIL AU 9 MAI 1960

avec des œuvres de :

BONA, BOUVIER, VICTOR BRAUNER, BRYEN, CAMACHO,
CARDENAS, CESAR, DADO, DUFOUR, FERRO, FAHLSTROM,
HARLOFF, HEROLD, HIQUILY, HUNDERTWASSER,
LAM, LEBEL, LICATA, MANINA, H. et P. MARTIN, MATTA,
HENRI MICHAUX, MONDINO, PEVERELLI, ANDRE-POUJET,
JACQUES PREVERT, SABY, TANCREDI, M. WATTEAU,
ENRIQUE ZANARTÜ.

avec le concours de :

D'EE, FRANÇOIS DUFRENE, JACKIE FARLEY,
MAX-POL FOUCHET, OCTAVIO PAZ,
ALLAN ZION et ANDRÉ PIEYRE DE MANDIARGUES.
ANNE LEANOR

Direction musicale : MAX HARSTEIN

POUR LE DROIT DE L'HOMME
A DISPOSER DE LUI-MÊME

« Quarante-deux Africains qui refusaient de plaider coupable ou non-coupable devant le Tri-bunal du Cap, comme la loi les y obligeait, ont déclaré : « Nous affirmons, pour le compte de la Communauté africaine, n'être sous aucune obligation morale d'obéir aux lois promulguées par une minorité étrangère blanche, qui légifère et administre le pays dans le seul but de nous opprimer et de sauvegarder ses propres intérêts. » (« France-Soir », 14-4-1960.)

En art, comme en politique, la MORALE n'a jamais servi qu'à justifier la coercition et l'arbitraire. Tous les hommes qui refusent de se soumettre aux lois de l'oppression, tous ceux qui se sont trouvés, ou qui se trouvent aujourd'hui, incarcérés pour délit de révolte contre le principe d'autorité, exaltent aussi la nécessité de la liberté de l'esprit. Toute réfutation de l'autorité morale du Maître est un acte révolutionnaire, un acte poétique, un acte de démystification.

Le but de la présente manifestation est d'affirmer la souveraineté du poète comme de l'artiste et leur désobéissance systématique à tous les dogmes. Mais souveraineté individuelle et solidarité ne sont pas inconciliables. L'internationalisme inhérent à la révolte s'oppose à toute conception nationaliste ou régionaliste de l'art. L'imputation de cosmopolitisme qui, venant des rédacteurs de l'*Humanité*, équivaut à une palinodie, alors qu'elle est dans la bonne tradition de l'*Action Française*, n'a rien de déshonorant pour nous, au contraire. Notre manifestation est, en son essence, intersubjective, cosmopolite dans sa forme.

En quoi consiste notre insoumission ?
En un refus de dissocier les moyens d'expression dont nous disposons.
En un refus de subordonner l'activité de l'esprit au commerce et à la propagande.
En un refus de respecter les idoles et les règles du jeu intellectuel.
En un refus de considérer le jugement moral autrement que comme une pratique anachronique et stérilisante.
En un refus de séparer la liberté de l'esprit de la liberté tout court.
Tout acte créateur est, d'abord, un anti-procès. Tout créateur est, jusqu'à nouvel ordre, un insoumis.

Paris, le 29 avril 1960

BONA, ROLAND BOUVIER, CARDENAS,
BERNARD DUFOUR, FRANÇOIS DUFRENE,
JACQUES GAMBIER DE LA FORTERIE,
MAX-POL FOUCHET, PHILIPPE HIQUILY,
ALAIN JOUFFROY, JEAN-JACQUES LEBEL,
ANDRÉ PIEYRE DE MANDIARGUES, MANINA,
ANDRE-POUJET, RENÉ DE SOLIER.

Un certain nombre de nos amis étrangers ont manifesté leur accord avec l'esprit de cette déclaration.

GALERIE DES QUATRE SAISONS

59, Rue de Grenelle, 59 —:— Paris-VI (Bab. 03-12)

Inauguration le VENDREDI 29 AVRIL 1960, à 21 h. 30

Les Imprimeurs Réunis de la Seine, 5, rue Git-le-Cœur, Paris-6e.

AUTO-DESTRUCTIVE ART

Demonstration by G. Metzger

SOUTH BANK LONDON 3 JULY 1961 11.45 a.m.—12.15 p.m.

Acid action painting. Height 7 ft. Length 12½ ft. Depth 6 ft. Materials: nylon, hydrochloric acid, metal. Technique. 3 nylon canvases coloured white black red are arranged behind each other, in this order. Acid is painted, flung and sprayed on to the nylon which corrodes at point of contact within 15 seconds.

Construction with glass. Height 13 ft. Width 9½ ft. Materials. Glass, metal, adhesive tape. Technique. The glass sheets suspended by adhesive tape fall on to the concrete ground in a pre-arranged sequence.

AUTO-DESTRUCTIVE ART

Auto-destructive art is primarily a form of public art for industrial societies.

Self-destructive painting, sculpture and construction is a total unity of idea, site, form, colour, method and timing of the disintegrative process.

Auto-destructive art can be created with natural forces, traditional art techniques and technological techniques.

The amplified sound of the auto-destructive process can be an element of the total conception.

The artist may collaborate with scientists, engineers.

Self-destructive art can be machine produced and factory assembled.

Auto-destructive paintings, sculptures and constructions have a life time varying from a few moments to twenty years. When the disintegrative process is complete the work is to be removed from the site and scrapped.

London, 4th November, 1959   *G. METZGER*

MANIFESTO AUTO-DESTRUCTIVE ART

Man in Regent Street is auto-destructive.
Rockets, nuclear weapons, are auto-destructive.
Auto-destructive art.
The drop drop dropping of HH bombs.
Not interested in ruins, (the picturesque)
Auto-destructive art re-enacts the obsession with destruction, the pummelling to which individuals and masses are subjected.
Auto-destructive art demonstrates man's power to accelerate disintegrative processes of nature and to order them.
Auto-destructive art mirrors the compulsive perfectionism of arms manufacture—polishing to destruction point.
Auto-destructive art is the transformation of technology into public art. The immense productive capacity, the chaos of capitalism and of Soviet communism, the co-existence of surplus and starvation; the increasing stock-piling of nuclear weapons—more than enough to destroy technological societies; the disintegrative effect of machinery and of life in vast built-up areas on the person,...

Auto-destructive art is art which contains within itself an agent which automatically leads to its destruction within a period of time not to exceed twenty years. Other forms of auto-destructive art involve manual manipulation. There are forms of auto-destructive art where the artist has a tight control over the nature and timing of the disintegrative process, and there are other forms where the artist's control is slight.
Materials and techniques used in creating auto-destructive art include: Acid, Adhesives, Ballistics, Canvas, Clay, Combustion, Compression, Concrete, Corrosion, Cybernetics, Drop, Elasticity, Electricity, Electrolysis, Electronics, Explosives, Feed-back, Glass, Heat, Human Energy, Ice, Jet, Light, Load, Mass-production, Metal, Motion Picture, Natural Forces, Nuclear energy, Paint, Paper, Photography, Plaster, Plastics, Pressure, Radiation, Sand, Solar energy, Sound, Steam, Stress, Terra-cotta, Vibration, Water, Welding, Wire, Wood.

London, 10 *March,* 1960   *G. METZGER*

AUTO-DESTRUCTIVE ART   MACHINE ART
AUTO CREATIVE ART

Each visible fact absolutely expresses its reality.

Certain machine produced forms are the most perfect forms of our period.

In the evenings some of the finest works of art produced now are dumped on the streets of Soho.

Auto creative art is art of change, growth movement.

Auto-destructive art and auto creative art aim at the integration of art with the advances of science and technology. The immidiate objective is the creation, with the aid of computers, of works of art whose movements are programmed and include "self-regulation". The spectator, by means of electronic devices can have a direct bearing on the action of these works.

Auto-destructive art is an attack on capitalist values and the drive to nuclear annihilation.

23 *June* 1961   *G. METZGER*

B.C.M. ZZZO London W.C.1.

Printed by St. Martins' Printers (TU) 86d, Lillie Road, London, S.W.6.

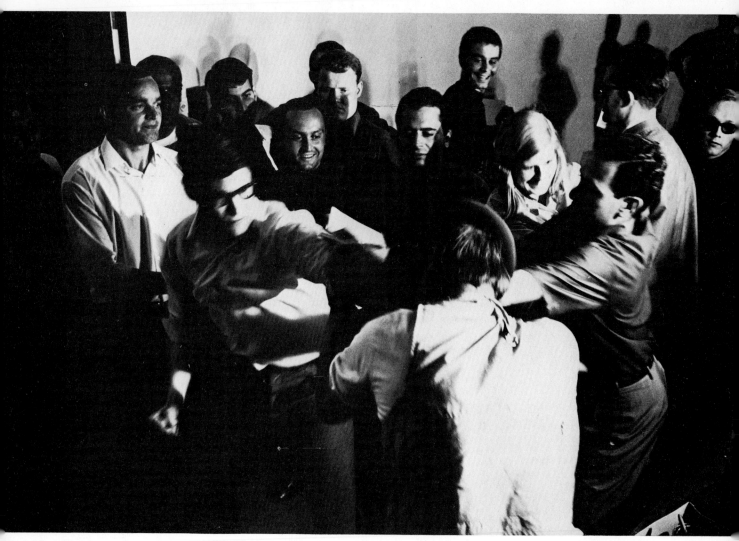

33

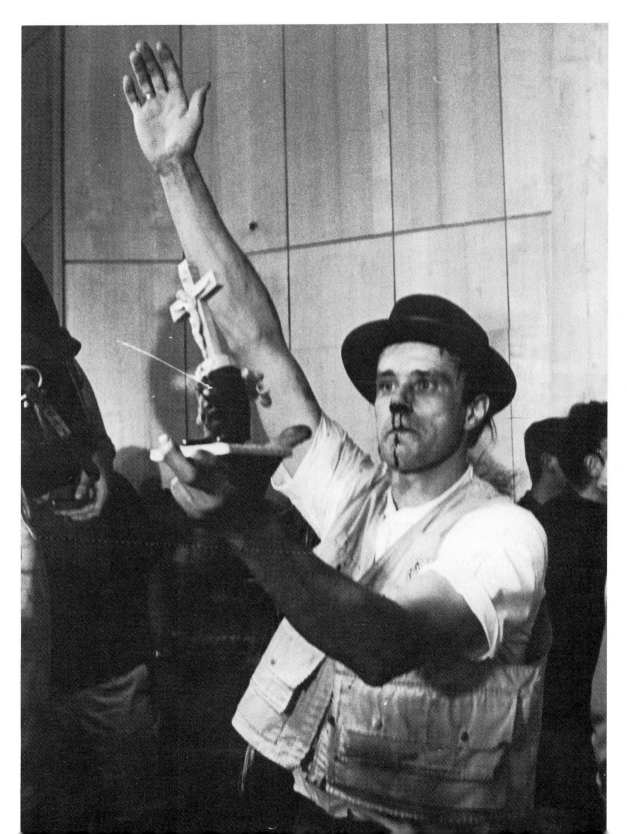

35

39

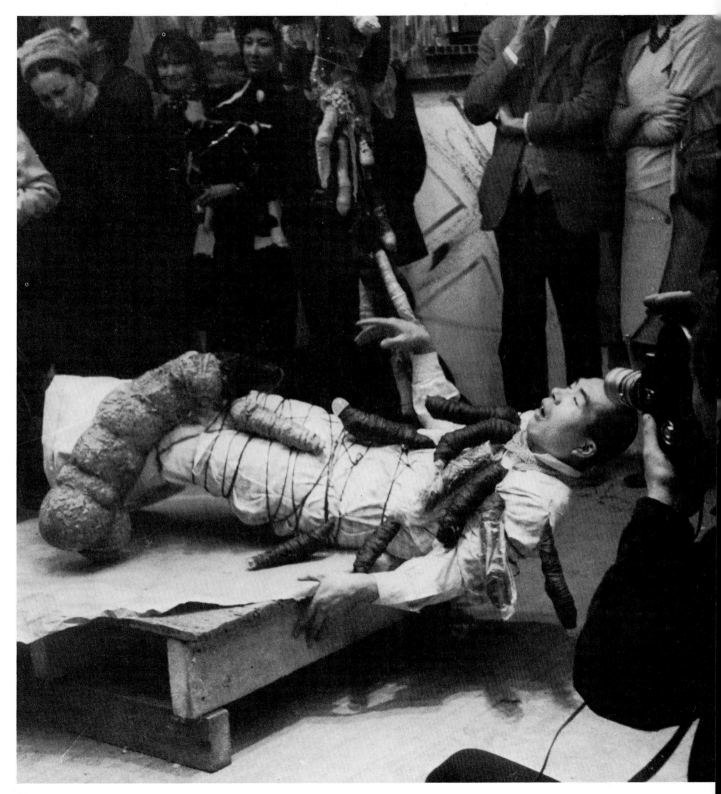

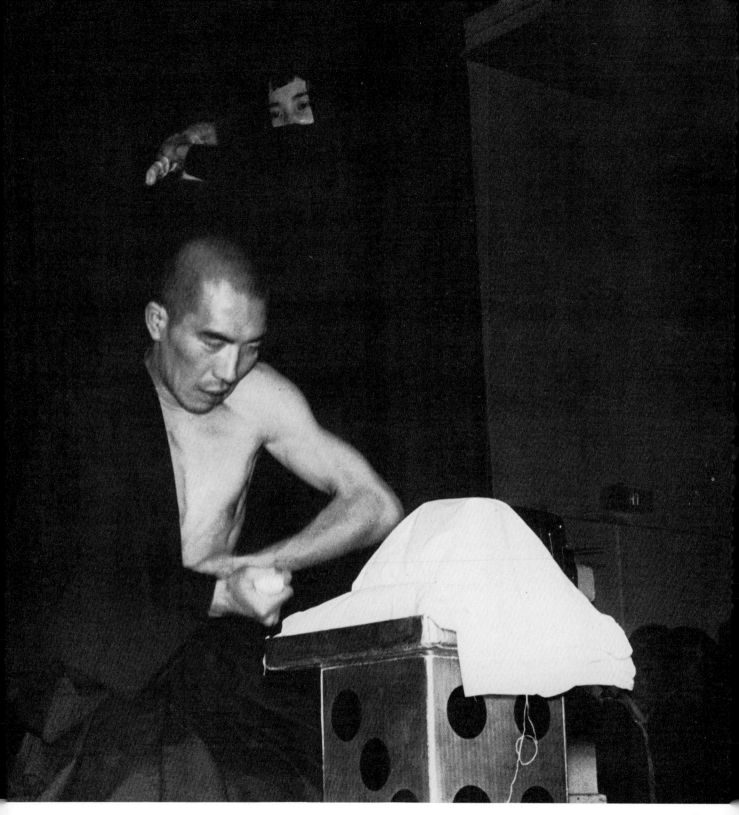

43

44

50

51

> "If the most unrelated things share a place, time, or odd similarity, there develop wonderful unities and peculiar relationships—and one thing reminds us of everything..."
>
> **Novalis**

2 Our discussion of the architecture, sculpture, and painting of the 1960s has revealed that boundaries between fields are being progressively disregarded, and that new forms have arisen in the interstices between disciplines (montage, assemblage, environmental art). This can also be seen in the sciences, where such interdisciplinary fields as biochemistry and astrophysics have proven their importance because they have led to completely new and often unexpected findings.

Such a development becomes truly striking when one looks at the arts in terms of time and space—poetry, music, theater, film and television, taken chronologically. Discoveries with countless consequences have been made in these arts, discoveries that can no longer be placed in traditional categories. An openness of almost ungraspable proportions has come into being, permitting, among other developments, a synthesis of the arts and sciences, which could have tremendous consequences for all areas of life. Probably the most important hybrid form in the sciences is cybernetics, which is called an "interscience." The term "interobject" has been introduced into information theory.

Obvious analogies to anti-classical epochs in the past come to mind, most compellingly the attempts at synesthesia characteristic of early German Romanticism, where dance, literature, and music were combined in one form. The borders between drama, fairy tale, novel, and poetry are often blurred in works of the Romantic period in Europe. And if boundaries are to be overcome in the arts, then they will sooner or later be overcome in the disciplines of art history. Nam June Paik wrote in 1967: "But if all the arts merge into one, as recent movements of mixed media show, then the study of various arts should merge too into one by the qualified investigator, who, if I may simulate Wiener, is a specialist in his own field but possesses a thoroughly sound and trained acquaintance with the fields of his neighbors."[52] This science of culture, which Paik quite rightly believes necessary, has only begun. The relationship between art and the stage is a venerable one.[53] Edward Gordon Craig's work comes immediately to mind, or the ballet "Relâche" by Picabia and Satie, or countless examples of Russian theater both before and after the Revolution. Artists like Picasso, Braque, Matisse, Gabo, Miro, Dali, Vasarely, Raysse, Accardi, Thek, and Israel have produced stage designs and sets and have contributed significantly to the marriage of disciplines. In the co-productions involving John Cage, Merce Cunningham's troupe, and such artists as Rauschenberg, Warhol, Johns, and Stella, music, dance, painting, and sculpture were integrated in such a balanced manner that the different powers of each medium worked independently to form a continually changing whole. One form did not serve another in the sense of being subordinate to it, but functioned freely in community with all the others. In other words, we are not talking about what John Cage called the "boom-boom relationship" of music to dance. Cage's music and texts are independent Happenings in themselves, the dance of Cunningham is movement in space parallel to Cage's music, and the works of Warhol, Stella, and Johns are also independent factors in the total theater experience.

Similarly, the Alwin Nikolais and Murray Louis dance groups make use of all the possibilities of this mutual interaction of media.[54] Light, fabrics, and moving bodies combine with the music in such a way that the total experience is almost extra-material. Just as architecture is no longer the dominating mother art of which all the other arts must be integral and subordinate parts, dance in this production no longer plays the dominant role—it is only one element. The films Ed Emshwiller made of performances by the Alwin Nikolais group, including "Totem" (1963) and "Fusions" (1967), are not only records but also independent works of film art. The freedom of each discipline is ensured, while concepts of new unities are born: acoustic with visual art, movement with stasis, material with ephemeral. The basis of this freedom is the new identity of life and art.

John Cage wrote: "Where other music and dance generally attempt to 'say' something, this theater is one that 'prevents' activity. It can be said to affirm life; to introduce an audience, not to a specialized world of art, but to the open, unpredictable changing world of everyday life."[55]

What Cage says here about Cunningham applies in even greater measure to Ann Halprin, who goes far beyond Cunningham in her dance-inspired Hap-

52 Norbert Weiner and Marshall McLuhan in ICA Bulletin, August–September, 1967.
53 Henning Rischbieter, ed., Bühne und bildende Kunst im XX. Jahrhundert, Velber bei Hannover, 1968; Merce Cunningham, Notes on Choreography, New York, 1968.
54 Marcia Siegel, "The Omniloquence of Alwin Nikolais," Dance Magazine, April, 1968.
55 John Cage in Arts and Society, 3, No. 2, p. 183.

penings.[56] Her work is an attempt to break down all barriers between aesthetics and the reality of life. For her, dance is no longer something to be "consumed" by the spectator, but something in which all should take part. The relationship of dance to architecture is very important to her, because she attempts to communicate a new and intensified feeling for the body and for movement—laws of tension for the real and the spatial—through sensual experience.

Ann Halprin's own words are revealing: "I am interested in a theater where everything is experienced as if for the first time, a theater of risk, spontaneity, exposure—and intensity. I want a partnership of the audience and the performer. I have stripped away all ties with conventional dance forms: the lives of the individual performers, the training, rehearsals, and the performances form a process in itself the experience. I have gone back to the ritualistic beginnings of art as a heightened expression of life. I wish to extend every kind of perception. I want to participate in events of supreme authenticity, to involve people with their environment so that life is lived whole."[57]

In such works as "Attic" and "Epitaph," Paul Taylor has introduced motionless dance and has thus reached the crucial culmination that forms a new point of departure, comparable to monochrome painting, monotone music (Yves Klein), the poem "Schweigen" ("Silence") by Eugen Gomringer, and the silent lecture (Cage and Ligeti).[58] The German Kaluza has worked out a dance whose effect depends on the relation between motion and motionlessness, which is also part of Alwin Nikolais's conception. The Dutch group BEWTH is trying to synchronize motion, space, architecture, and music. In his more recent work, "Slouching Toward Bethlehem," for example, Don Redlich is working toward provocatively sensitive actions. Yvonne Rainer, especially in her work with Robert Morris, has crossed the border into the Happening, in that the arts of motion and the static arts, the time arts and the space arts, flow together in her compositions into one.

Dance, theater, film, painting, sculpture, architecture, music, literature—all have been combined into a new unity, called by as neutral a name as possible, to avoid associations with any one field of art: the Happening.[59] This word suggests the authentic character of such events and their basis in everyday life. The Happening, a synthesis, is a continuation of the stream of art, previously divided into so many branches. Allan Kaprow visualizes the possibility of collecting so much material into three-dimensional montages or assemblages that the observer can enter them, become elements in in them, and change them at will.[60]

56   Ann Halprin, "What and How I Believe," Art's and Society, Spring–Summer, 1968; Ann Halprin, "Mutual Creation," Tulane Drama Review, Fall, 1968.
57   Ann Halprin in Arts and Society, Spring–Summer, 1968, pp. 58–59.
58   Udo Kultermann, "Die Sprache des Schweigens," Quadrum, 20, 1966.
59   Udo Kultermann, "Was ist ein Happening?" Die Tat (Zurich), August 26, 1967.
60   Allan Kaprow, Assemblage, Environments und Happenings, New York, 1967.

So, once again, Happenings are art events comprised of color, light, space, movement, sounds, noises, shapes, and more. Artists who make Happenings take fragments of reality out of context, create new interrelationships with them, and transform them, using apparently arbitrary parameters, into a process that usually seems illogical, yet is very often aesthetically satisfying. Joseph Beuys replied to a journalist who asked him why he used language meant to shock its hearers: "My language is not meant to shock. It's a precise, often intense statement, which, because is it anti-art and/or art, requires that the audience be quite imaginative." Allan Kaprow, Robert Whitman, Red Grooms, Claes Oldenburg, Jim Dine, Nam June Paik, Tetsumi Kudo, Otto Mühl, Hermann Nitsch, Joseph Beuys, and many others have staged Happenings—aesthetic events that take place in the context of reality. They excite emotions and create forms that can no longer be taken apart with the toolset of conventional aesthetics. Perhaps even more important, the Happening is a form that cannot be put into an economic category; it cannot be exploited for profit, and this is sociologically and politically significant.

Some of the earliest Happenings took place in Japan.[61] They were planned by a group of artists who met in Osaka, called themselves Gutai, and rented an old warehouse for art exhibitions and events. The earliest documentation on the Gutai group dates from 1956. The significant features of the Happening were already in evidence here: the incorporation of media conventionally thought of as extra-aesthetic, the extension of the work into the surrounding space, and the melting together of different areas of art, where the artist, instead of letting his work speak for him, comes out in front of it and becomes an actor. For an open-air exhibition in a pine woods at Ashyia City near Kobe, the Gutai artists built huge figures after designs by Atsuko Tanaka and lighted them from the inside with strings of colored lamps. The lamps flashed rhythmically, suggesting such disparate effects as outdoor advertising and blood circulation. A moving strip covered with footprints snaked across the forest floor and up a tree. There were also spatial constructions that could be entered, traffic signs, jellyfish-shaped mounds of mud, plastic, and rope, stuffed sacks hanging from trees tied with ribbons. In the same year Saburo Murakami staged "Struggling with the Screen," a Happening that involved an element later to be repeated in similar events all over the world: breaking and jumping through paper walls.

In July of 1957 the Gutai group presented its first Happening in a theater, called "Gutai Art on the Stage." The amateur documentary films made there show figures in masks and fantastic costumes in a interplay of masquerade and strip show. They used spotlights, billows of smoke, fire, water, and incandescent light; they blew up balloon after balloon and popped them. The third theatrical presentation by the Gutai group, given in the Sankai Hall in Osaka

61 Udo Kultermann, "Happenings Wiege stand in Osaka," Artis, January, 1966; M. Cohen, "Japan's Gutai Group," Art in America, November–December, 1968.

in 1962, included Happenings called "Dance for Rock," "Faces and Signs," and "Turning Silver Wall."

More recent Happenings were staged by Kuniharu Akiyama, Toshi Ichiyanagi and Toru Takemitsu.[62] Ichiyanagi's "Experimental Music" was part of a Happening staged in 1966 in the Sogetsu Art Center in Tokyo. Takemitsu presented his "Blue Aurora for Toshi Ichiyanagi" at the East–West Festival in Hawaii in 1964.

The Happening in Austria has gained its specific character from the work of Otto Mühl, Günter Brus, and Hermann Nitsch, who came to the theater from Action Painting.[63] Mühl called his Happenings "material actions": "a 'material action' is painting grown outside the bounds of the canvas plane; a human body, a table laid for dinner where the "material happening" takes place, or a 'space'—they all become the picture plane. The dimensions of the body and the dimensions of space are joined by the dimension of time: the sequence of actions, their speed, the simultaneity of several actions. The theater usually still works with symbols that are in themselves the story. They don't try to explain anything, they are what they seem to be and what they look like... reality in the process of becoming." He reaches the conclusion: "The 'material action' is a method of expanding reality, of creating new realities and of widening the dimensions of experience."

Hermann Nitsch also came from painting to the Happening. Since 1961, his work has been based on and driven by "that immemorial excess, the mangled lamb." In the manifesto he published for the Venice Biennale in 1964 he attempted to define his terms: "a more conscious, expanded, sensitive, sensuous perception of the environment combines itself with the perception of the symbolic content inherent in every concrete object or concrete process; in other words, every conceivable association that, through art, dissolves the areas of reality it quotes, is imbued with life, systematically broken down, and given over to consciousness." Nitsch believes that "the concrete objects utilized are only ciphers of an inner psychic reality that can be dredged down to archetypal collective basic prerequisites of mind."[64]

Allan Kaprow, in the course of the numerous Happenings he has staged since the 1950s, has progressively eliminated the audience. "Calling," 1965, had no public, only participants. They began in different parts of New York City, their activities took them through various boroughs on different paths, and they all ended up in a woods in New Jersey. The Happening could not be seen as a whole by any one of the participants, not even Kaprow himself. Even so, according to Michael Kirby, who took part in "Calling," the fact that each individual knew the basic conception made the Happening an aesthetic whole

62 Roger Reynolds, "Happenings in Japan and Elsewhere," Arts and Society, Spring-Summer, 1968.
63 Udo Kultermann, "Pop und Hap, die realisierte Dynamik in der zeitgenössischen Kunst, "Artis, 3, 1965,
64 G. Zacharias, Satanskult und Schwarze Messe, Wiesbaden, 1964,

in each person's mind during his activity, through association. Kirby says also that, during the short pre-Happening conference with Kaprow in a bar, everybody suddenly had the feeling that everything they were saying and doing was already part of the "play." Life and art intermingled: "Activities, by their very nature, can exploit the possibility of fusion with everyday life more directly and easily than any other art form."[65]

The powers of imagination released during events like this often not easily analyzed; there is much that cannot be rationally decoded; there is an ever-present risk of failure,—and that is why Happenings touch closer to the heart of the human situation in our time than any other form of contemporary art. Happenings create concrete relationships where there were only abstract ones before; they are a significant aesthetic contribution to our perception of the reality of the here and now.

Another facet of the intermedia was developed by Peter Dockley with the combinations of dance, gymnastics, music, and objects he presented in London from September 22 to 29, 1969. He designed both the masks and scaffolding himself, and the production was announced in the following manner: "An open-form theater piece with gymnasts, acrobats, kendo, smoke, tubes, event-costumes, Soft Machine, Indian musicians. The openstaging is a series of interconnecting structures focused in the center of the Roundhouse space and extending to the edges of the circle. With mobile audience."

"Instrumental theater" is Heinz Klaus Metzger's name for the combination of music with theater worked out on the basis of primitive forms found in jazz, especially by John Cage, Mauricio Kagel, and György Ligeti. Paolo Scheggi attempted to fuse literature and action in a new way in his "interventi plastico-visuali" in the Piccolo Teatro in Milan in 1968; Ferdinand Kriwet presents his poems visually. In their book "Roman" ("Novel"), Peter O. Chotjewitz and Gunter Rambow used photos and text as structural building blocks. C. Parmiggiani and A. Spatola wanted to inundate the town of Fiumalbo with poetry in their Happening, "Parole sui Mure," 1967. The program included F. Tiziano declaring himself to be a poem: "Io sono una poesia." Jean–Jacques Lebel brought literature to the nude model in "Les Femmes Collages," one part of the Happening "Pour Conjurer l'Esprit de Catastrophe," performed in 1963.

Not only has the theater incorporated many of the effects of painting, it is in the process of making the film a legitimate element of its art.[66] Among the numerous experiments of this kind are the Laterna Magica in Prague and works by Robert Whitman and Milton Cohen. Robert Rauschenberg's contribution to the "Nine Evenings" in the Armory in 1966, "Open Score," included 300 people in the darkened hall being filmed by infrared television cameras.

65 Michael Kirby, The Art of Time, New York, 1969, pp. 165 ff.
66 Michael Kirby, "The Uses of Film in the New Theater," Tulane Drama Review, XI, No. 1, 1966, pp. 49–61.

The films were projected on huge screens scattered around the huge room. In "Dance for One Figure, Four Objects and Film Sequence," Don Redlich contrasted filmed dance with the live dancing on the stage. Stage reality and filmic reproduction were also successfully combined in Kenneth Tynan's musical "Oh! Calcutta!," 1969.

Painting, sculpture, and other visual arts can be merged with film, as Robert Whitman's "Cinema Pieces" show. Marcel Broodthaers fused literature and film by projecting films on a screen covered with words. Contemporary experiments that blur the barrier between poetry and music—whose tradition goes back to the Middle Ages and ancient Greece—are exemplified by Hans G. Helms's spoken music, Mauricio Kagel's staged music, music as Happening ("Originale" by Karlheinz Stockhausen), or by the use of silence.

For "Myth Atonement" Ann Halprin had an environment made of newspapers function as a place of meditation, where the participants sat silently for an hour surrounded by the sounds of drums and then expressed their thoughts in concise form—two words maximum. She described it thus: "This was like the ordeals in primitive initiation rites. It was a time for self-examination and meditation upon sin—whatever that word may mean to modern man." And she added that during this event she felt as if she were experiencing theater for the first time.[67] The participants in another Happening, "Expositions," carried blank protest signs up and down Market Street in San Francisco. The opinions of the confused onlookers were recorded on tape.

The extent to which music is significant in the combining of previously separate media is shown by the key role played by a composer like John Cage. He not only had a great influence on the visual arts of the 1950s and 1960s, but also on theater, dance, literature, and other fields. Yannis Xenakis conceived an electronic poem combining music, space, and moving pictures for the Philips Pavilion of the Brussels Worlds Fair of 1958. Xenakis worked with Le Corbusier, who designed the Pavilion. Steve Reich very recently developed new forms of music from a rhythmic montage of spoken and sung texts ("It's Gonna Rain").

The work of Nam June Paik has also been an important stimulus since the second half of the 1950s, when he began presenting his Happening-like music-theater compositions, first in Germany and later in America. Paik, perhaps more than anyone else, has staked out his claim in intermedia. His word-symphonies and his staged compositions, like the works of the Fluxus group (La Monte Young, George Maciunas, Robert Filliou, Dick Higgins, George Brecht) and Ben Patterson's paper symphonies, have only recently been recognized for what they are—predecessors of an art of conceptions. Paik's "Young Penis Symphony" or the "Danger Music for Dick Higgins," which includes the stage direction "Creep into vagina of a living female whale," and his other compositions of words, movements, noises, tones, colors, smells, etc., fuse every area together with mysterious, non-decodable significance

67   J. Anderson, "The Material of Myths," Dance Magazine, April, 1968.

that is so intense and aggressive that the audience cannot help but be provoked or engaged.

In 1961 Paik wrote a symphony for twenty rooms; in order to realize the artist's conception, the audience had to go from room to room and hear the music in a variety of infinite permutations and sequences. Physical movement suddenly assumed an important role for the person accustomed solely to listening to music. Instruments were provided for anyone who wanted to make music himself. Paik's goal is to reactivate the senses by "combining many senses: touching, blowing, caressing, seeing, treading, walking, running, hearing, striking, etc."

Together with Charlotte Moorman, the cellist, Paik entered the field of television a few years ago, in an attempt to generate active involvement in a medium conventionally experienced only passively. In the color television sets devised by Paik, the movements of the viewer influence the changing picture on the screen, thus introducing a new kind of relationship between the viewer and the apparatus. Paik wrote the opera "Opera Sextonique" for Charlotte Moorman; she plays it in attitudes that are events in themselves, often nude from the waist up, often wearing a bra made of two miniature television sets. Such transmusical moments are common in the work of Paik and contribute to its uniqueness.

In his "Originale," played for the first time in Cologne in 1961, Karlheinz Stockhausen brought together the disciplines of music, literature, visual art, and pantomime. The piece was performed in New York in September, 1964, with Kaprow, Robert Breer, Strider, Ginsberg, Jackson MacLow, Lette Eisenhauer, Billy Klüver, Higgins, and others.

This discussion can touch on only a small part of all the activities designed to break down the barriers between media. Yves Klein, who wrote a one-tone symphony, and Piero Manzoni have already begun musical experiments. The Baschet brothers and Attilio Pierilli created sonorous sculptures, Gregorio Vardanega built light and movement producing apparatus. Howard Jones's paintings combine photocells with speakers to activate the spectator. Perhaps the most comprehensive of all in unifying different media was David Medalla's "Exploding Galaxy" in London, which addressed itself to all the senses.

In the arts all over the world the thousand ways of creating an effect aesthetically are coming together to form one broad panorama; one medium no longer serves another or is subordinate to it—each retains its independence or merges totally with the other to form a new medium. Artists are finally breaking down the wall between the work and the observer, between art and life. In every case, we are challenged to take part, to become engaged.

53

55

57

59

60

63

64

94

UNDERGROUND
CONST. CO.

"I want to participate in events of supreme authenticity,
to involve people with their environment so that
life is lived whole."

Ann Halprin

3 Bridging the psychic distance between the work of art and the observer's frame of reference, be it gallery or concert hall, and whether the spectator is looking at the framed painting or a sculpture on a pedestal, is a problem of much concern in contemporary culture, and by no means limited to the arts.

The taboos we inherited from another era—the rituals of bourgeois society—are no longer valid today. New rituals are now evolving. Ann Halprin describes her conception of the work "Myths" (1967): "'Myths' resulted from my desire to evolve a method of setting the groundwork for the spontaneous release of feelings and movements through which could be developed the re-enactment of archetypal community rites."[68]

The open ended nature of processes, the manipulability of objects, the reactivation of every individual's creativity—even individual responsibility itself—are concepts that symbolize the transformation contemporary culture is undergoing. The student protest movements with all their "techniques" are just as representative as staged political happenings.[69] They too can be defined in terms of the concepts listed above. Self-immolation as political demonstration (Quang Duc in Saigon, Norman Morrison in Washington, Jan Palach in Prague)—symbolic politics—is the logical consequence of personal engagement in society.

In the visual arts, tendencies toward mobility, kinetics, and audience participation originated long before the 1960s. Alexander Calder's mobiles can be set in motion by a touch of the finger as well as by a breath of wind. Other

68 Ann Halprin, "Mutual Creation," Tulane Drama Review, Fall, 1968.
69 R. Kinteh, Rebellion, New York, 1968; N. O'Gorman, ed., Revolution, New York, 1968. 101

important steps away from a fixed, final, and object-oriented art toward an art that is open, variable, and manipulable—toward art as play—were taken by Yaacov Agam, Jean Tinguely, Nicholas Schöffer, Bruno Munari, Julio Le Park, Len Lye, Oyvind Fahlström, Hanlor, Newton, Harrison, and many others.[70] Piero Manzoni built a scultura vivente, where anyone who likes can climb up on the pedestal, place his feet on the marks painted for them, and consider himself a work of art. Ay-O built boxes and walls with holes and apertures that provide various interesting sensations for the fingers placed into them. Dieter Hacker made pictures to be played with, and even eaten, and a kinetic room (1964). Elio Marchegiani's work "Venus" consists of a large box that automatically takes a person's picture as soon as he enters it.

Participation is a key word in works that make use of the elemental things in nature, such as Hans Haacke's water and air sculptures and Bernard Aubertin's fire pictures and fire books. The user can strike a match to them whenever he feels like it. This kind of art can be made of found objects or prefabricated parts. It can be changed and altered; it is an object not for posterity, but one to be used just like any other object in our lives—to satisfy momentary desires.

The same is true of works designed to activate sense perception. Lygia Clark, with her touch-objects, suits of clothes, caps, hoods, and environments wants only to make people conscious that they are equipped with perfectly good senses, if they would only use them. Being an observer is not enough to experience or to enjoy this work—one has to hear, smell, feel, seek, and sharpen one's senses. Lygia Clark's articles of clothing are not works of art in the old sense. Their goal is to provoke the sensorium into functioning, to activate the whole man.

"Why Not: A Serenade of Eschatological Ecology" (1969), a film by Arakawa, is based on a similar conception; it shows a girl relating to objects physically and sensually. Similarly, Ann Halprin had students of architecture demonstrate and experience with their own bodies the laws of tension, dynamics, and loading.

Nor are Franz Erhard Walther's usable—and useful—objects works to be looked at only: "These objects are instruments and mean little when you look at them. It is not the objects that are important, but what happens with them, what it is possible to do with them." And he added later: "We, the users, have to do the job. Our skills (or lack of them) and our movements count."[71] A comparison might be drawn with the dance masks of African natives, temporary instruments that gained their significance and function in the ritual of the dance itself; Walther's objects are simply tools with which the user produces an aesthetic experience. The new perspectives of this art are

70 F. Popper, Naissance de l'art cinétique, Paris, 1967; Jack Burnham, Beyond Modern Sculpture, New York, 1968.

71 Germano Celant, Art Povera. New York, 1969, p. 174.

particularly apparent in the case of objects designed for use by several people at once—doing, a social process, is at the center of it.

In "Masks," part one of "Myth" (1967), Ann Halprin had partners explore each other's faces with their fingertips, eyes closed. In "Paper Dance" the participants come into direct physical contact with an environment made entirely of paper.

Technological innovations bring with them many new possibilities. Here, too, the use of the most highly developed techniques has led to a re-evaluation of the human element, especially the constants of our physical existence. This is well demonstrated by Howard Jones's works, in which the presence of a person in front of one of his objects is enough to trigger a photocell, transforming the subtlest movement into sound. This makes the observer active in a new sense. Jones said the following about his work "Sonic Seven" (1968–69): "I wanted to (put) emphasis on the spectator, the person witnessing, the participator. On the surface of this negated square is a group of five equidistant photo conductors, making the corners of a square and the point in the center. The layout is designed to receive the human body. The spectator, in his movement before the piece, interrupts the beam of light and the work resounds with diversified electronic pitches. Each movement produces a frequency, and by varying position or motions, one can create an unlimited number of linear sound patterns." A decade ago the painter Georges Mathieu danced in the process of painting; Jones is the organizer and choreographer who makes the "user" of his work into a dancer.

In Robert Rauschenberg's "Soundings" (1969), the observer, through sounds made either consciously or unconsciously, activates contacts that light up particular parts of the composition.

Marta Minujin's "Minuphone" (1967) is a telephone booth in which, when someone makes a call, colored water climbs between the double glass wall of the booth, wind blows in the caller's face, and his own picture appears on closed-circuit television—he participates directly in the aesthetic process.[72]

For "Minucode" (1968) Marta Minujin filmed a cocktail party. The films are projected on the walls of an empty room so that anyone in the room feels himself a part of the event. One could rent these films to liven up a real party or even buy them and surround oneself with one's own private cocktail party. Other important environments in which the spectator may choose to play the role of participant were made by Robert Whitman ("Vibrating Mirror Room," 1968), Stanley Landsman ("Walk-In Infinite Chamber," 1968), and Boyd Mefferd and Hans Haacke ("Photo-Electric Viewer Programmed Coordinate System," 1968).

In Keiji Usami's Laser-Beam-Environment, people moving in the room create constantly changing groupings of different colored laser beams. Here participation is a function of physical presence. Jean Dupuy's "Heart Beat Machine" makes the user's heartbeat visible on a screen. Here participation becomes

72 Michael Kirby, "Marta Minujin's Simultaneity," Tulane Drama Review, Spring, 1968.

a kind of magical ceremony that, although it is based in reality, creates a reality that could not, up to now, be optically experienced.

Similar intensions inform the products of artists working in television, a medium generally thought to condemn its audience to a degree of passivity unparalleled by any other. Such artists as Paik, Levine, Warhol, Tambellini, Thomas Tadlock, Siegel, and Walther de Maria have all investigated the creative possibilities inherent in this, the most socially powerful of media.[73] Television offers multiple frames of reference in place of linear thought, a multidimensionality that represents a challenge to activity, but at the cost of the loss of continuity. Discontinuity is one of the most pregnant characteristics of television, the same discontinuity that has influenced all areas of life.

Film has not been left out of artists' attempts to stimulate participation in their audience, as shown by the Czech experiment in which the audience was given the chance to decide by majority vote how the film was to end, or by Stephen Dwoskin's "Take Me" (1968), in which the actor talks directly to the audience.

As noted above, Nam June Paik has concentrated on television perhaps more than any other artist, either giving the user of his objects the chance to communicate his movements through photocells to the screen, or by manipulating the televised image through hand-held electromagnets, which cause disturbances of a similar kind. Works of art here are objects for play, like pinball machines or one-armed bandits.

In his work "Contact" of 1969, Les Levine brought nine TV monitors and four TV cameras together into a cybernetic sculpture that shows to the observer his own image from continually changing points of view: close-ups, long shots, varying camera angles. He also provided a tentative theoretical basis for the new aesthetic possibilities of TV: "Television has given us a totally different idea of focus the same way as photography changed our way of looking at images in relationship to the way we paint them. Television has made multiple focus acceptable; as a result we can see many different focal planes at once."[74] In Paul Ryan's "Everyman's Möbius Strip" anyone from the public can take his own picture with a TV camera and then play the results back in private. Ryan commented thus on his experiment: "A Möbius Strip is a one-sided surface made by taking a long rectangular paper, giving it a half twist, and joining its ends. Any two points on the strip can be connected by starting at one point and tracing a line to the other without crossing over a boundary of lifting the pencil. The outside is the inside. The inside is the outside. Here the power of videotaped recorder (VTR) is used to take in our own outside. When you see yourself on tape, you are seeing the image you are presenting to the world. When you see yourself watching yourself on tape, you are seeing

73   John S. Margolies, "TV–The Next Medium," Art in America, September–October, 1969.
74   Les Levine in Art in America, September–October, 1969, p. 50.

your real self, your 'inside.'... The Möbius tapestrip snips the barrier between inside and outside. It offers you one continuous 'sur'-face with nothing to hide.[75]

While his picture is being taken, the user is given suggestions in the artist's voice recorded on tape. One is completely alone during the shooting and replay and can erase the videotape images immediately afterward. Here the term "observer" has a much more sublimated meaning than ever before. As in these experiments with television and the dance events of Ann Halprin, in which there is no longer any differentiation made between professional dancers and their layman audiences, the participation of everyone concerned is also especially important for today's theater. The Bengali peasant revolts of 1968 were set off by a revolt played on the stage and directed at precisely the effect on reality it had. In the Minerva Theater on Beadon Street in Calcutta, the play "Teer" ("Arrow") by Uptal Dutta was performed. Dutta, an actor, producer, author, and Maoist in one, had his players decide to organize against the landowners and collectivize the land. Again, theater became the model for reality—the peasants seized upon the situation played on stage and actually carried out the revolt. As opposed to the ideological, didactic plays of European origin, theater in the third world has a very real function. Likewise, the occupation of the Théâtre de l'Odéon was a logical consequence of the street demonstrations of the Paris uprisings of 1968.

A pioneer in changing the function of theater was the Pole Jerzy Grotowski with his Polish Lab-Theater.[76] He began developing his conception in 1959 and continued and expanded it when he came to New York in 1967. Grotowski, who strives for what he calls "poor theater," made an early case for the participation of the audience and the interaction of stage and observer's space. Eugenio Barba, himself head of a theater in Holstebro, Denmark, and involved in the renewal of the art, said of Grotowski: "Grotowski often speaks of 'theatrical magic.' What he means is that an actor worthy of the name must be able to perform physical and vocal feats beyond the ability of the spectator. He is a sorcerer, who enthralls the spectator. He must force the spectator outside of himself and make him part of the dramatic action—an action that is no longer narrowly limited by the stage and that necessitates a new rapport between actors and spectators united in the creation of the world. In the Theater Laboratory the spectators are made to face the most secret, the most carefully hidden parts of themselves."[77]

Peter Brook wrote of Grotowski: "So that the act of performance, of sacrificing what most men prefer to hide—this sacrifice is his gift to the spectator. Grotowski's actors offer their performance as a ceremony for those who

75 Exhibition catalogue, "TV as a Creative Medium," Howard Wise Gallery, New York, May 17–June 14, 1969.
76 Jerzy Grotowski, Toward a Poor Theater, New York, 1969.
77 Eugenio Barba, Alla ricerca del teatro perduto, Padua, 1965; Jerzy Grotowski, Toward a Poor Theater, New York, 1969.

wish to assist: the actor invokes, lays bare what lies in every man—and what daily life covers up."[78]

Among the groups performing in America are Julian and Judith Beck's Living Theater, Ellen Stewart's La Mama Troup, Richard Schechner's Performance Group and Joseph Chaikin's Open Theater. The Living Theater has provided the model for the others, with its lack of traditional actors, stage decor, and costumes.[79] Its goal is the total identity of art and life. Its theater is a model situation, a societal process. With their theater work, which includes street theater, the Becks want to confront total reality with one phase of itself that is more harmonious than the rest. During the performance of "Paradise Now" (1968) audience participation was strong in many countries; actors and spectators alike made trance-like, ritual contact, which hinted at many new possibilities—and not only for the theater.

In newer pieces for the theater—in America, above all—the attempts made to include the audience in the performance have gone quite far, as far as an invitation to lovemaking, in many cases. John Lahr[80] describes how, in one case, actors came down from the stage and tried their best to make intimate contact with persons in the audience, programmatically: "The actors are playing, but their drama is more a matter of life and death. 'We are at Daytop because there is no refuge, finally, from ourselves.' The players scream, weep, agonize in loneliness and despair. At the conclusion, these isolated individuals, feared within the community, ostracized as forces of social disorder rather than products of it, step out to the audience and speak to anyone who will look them in the eye: 'I want you to love me. Please.' They embrace members of the audience." The piece is called "The Conquest."

"Tiempo de fregar," also a work created collectively by all the players involved (it was presented in 1969 in the Centro de Experimentation Autovisial del Instituto Torquato di Tella in Buenos Aires), is similarly concerned with a new mutual interaction of actors with their audience. As the spectators enter the theater the players dance with them, in a dance that progresses in intensity as the evening goes on until erotic contact is made. Here too, authenticity of experience replaces theater art in the traditional sense as the prime goal.

Just as in the very popular "Hair" performances, these theater events want the spectator to double as a player, to take part in theater as life, rather than to attend a theater that simulates life. Thus the examples I have listed no longer fit the schemes defined by our aesthetic legacies.

The participation of actors and audience, artist and society, in an all-encompassing event is analogous to political reality. To reform society—and this is

78 Eugenio Barba and L. Flaszen, "A Theater of Magic and Sacrilege," Tulane Drama Review, IX, No. 3, pp. 173–174; Peter Brook, The Empty Space, New York, 1968, pp. 59 ff.
79 Erika Billeter, The Living Theater, Paradise Now, Bern, 1968; P. Biner, Le Living Théâtre, Lausanne, 1968.
80 John Lahr, "The New Theater in America," London Magazine, December, 1968; John Lahr, "The Theater's Voluptuary Itch," London Magazine, April, 1969.

necessary—requires participation. The prerequisites for individual participation, however, are many: a sense of responsibility, the ability to think
independently, and the will not to let oneself be manipulated, driven, or
coerced. These abilities are at present underdeveloped. Most people are quite
satisfied with the bourgeois system, supported by the pillars of the police and
the military and exuding the ethos of consumption and double morality, even
though, as the Surrealists accused their contemporaries as early as 1925, "the
barracks and prisons being built today are like daily bread to you—such
monstrosities don't surprise you any more." They defined catastrophe like
this: "Catastrophe? That would be if a world where people pass judgment on
people continued to exist."

Whereas the Dadaists and Surrealists worked through shock and scandal to
épater le bourgeois—that is, towards changing society mentally—today's
artist works with actions that challenge participation by the whole person,
body, mind, and senses. That is the basic difference between contemporary
Happenings and Dadaist and Surrealist thinking and action, without which,
it must be said, society would not have changed in the ways it has. The artist
is no longer working cut off from society, he is looking for ways to act within
it. His goal is to unify his work with society, to give up his traditional class
status. He sees the new function in engagement, in making ideas effective,
the way a shaman does. Esoteric brusqueness and contempt for his audience
is no longer part of the show. To a remark made by Wolf Vostell that the
audience reacted badly in one of his Happenings, the Czech Milan Knizak
replied, justifiably: "There is no such thing as a poor reaction of participants,
but there can be a 'poor Happening.'" The phenomenon of participation
mirrors the general desire of artists to regain their function in the community,
to become an effective part of society, a group capable in itself of making
society as a whole more productive and creative.

75

76

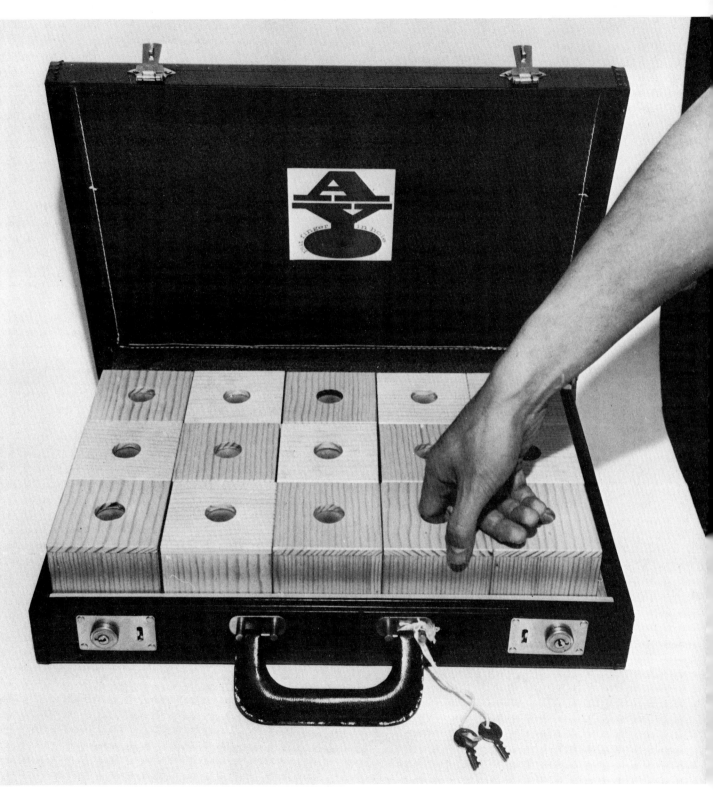

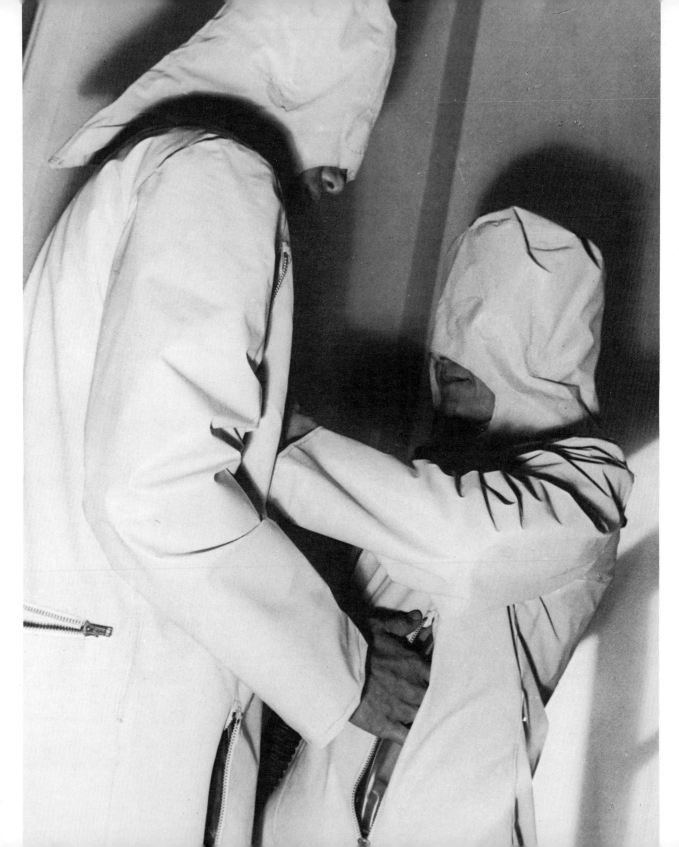

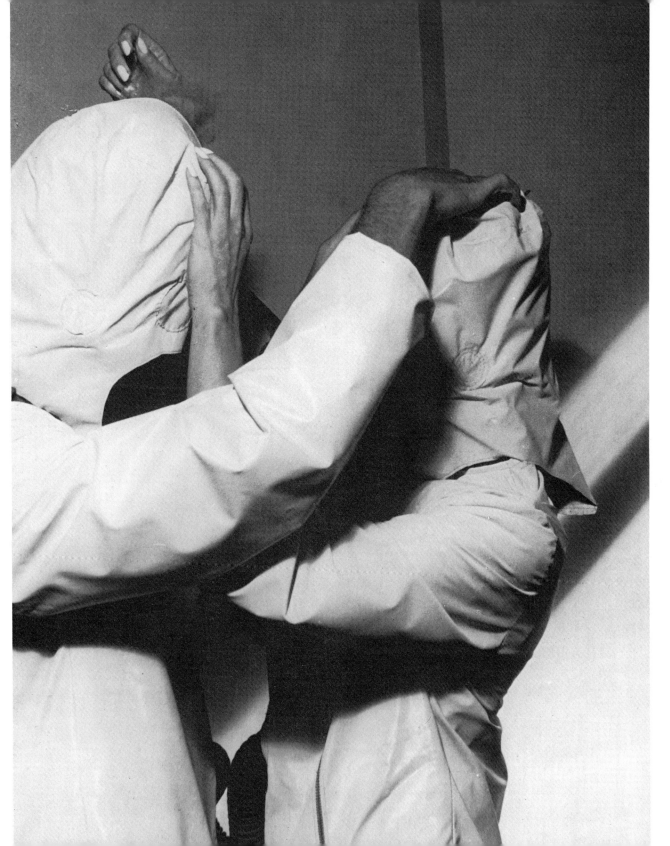

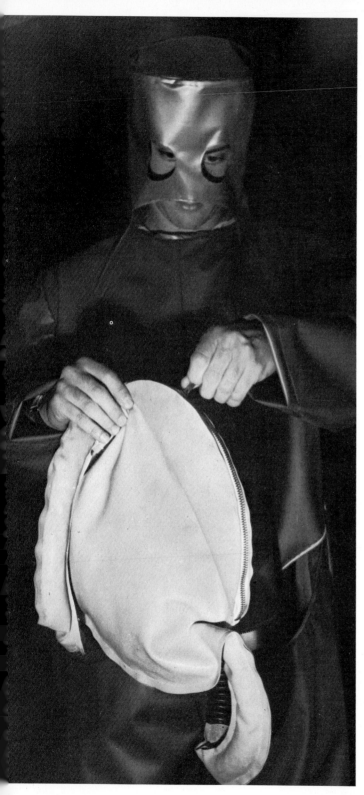

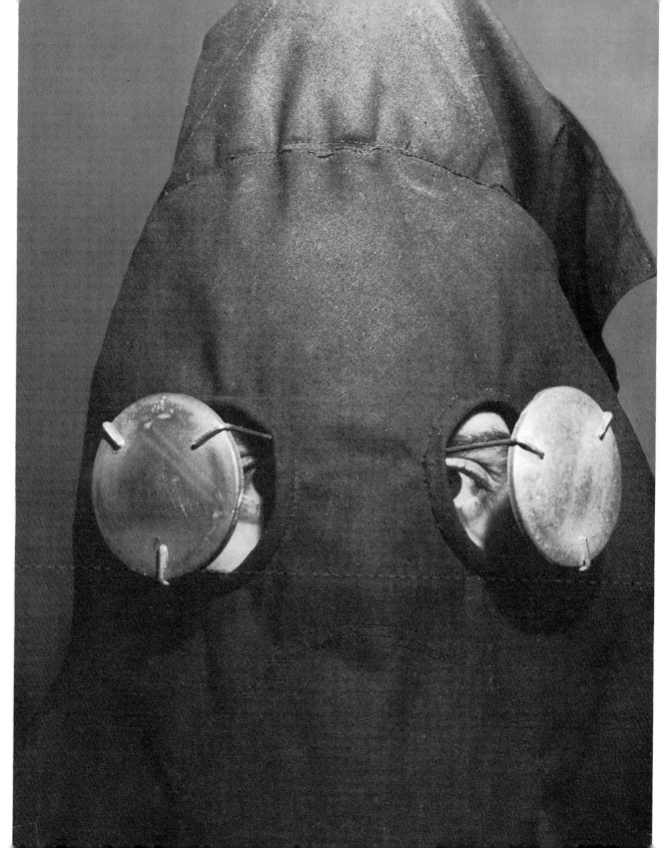

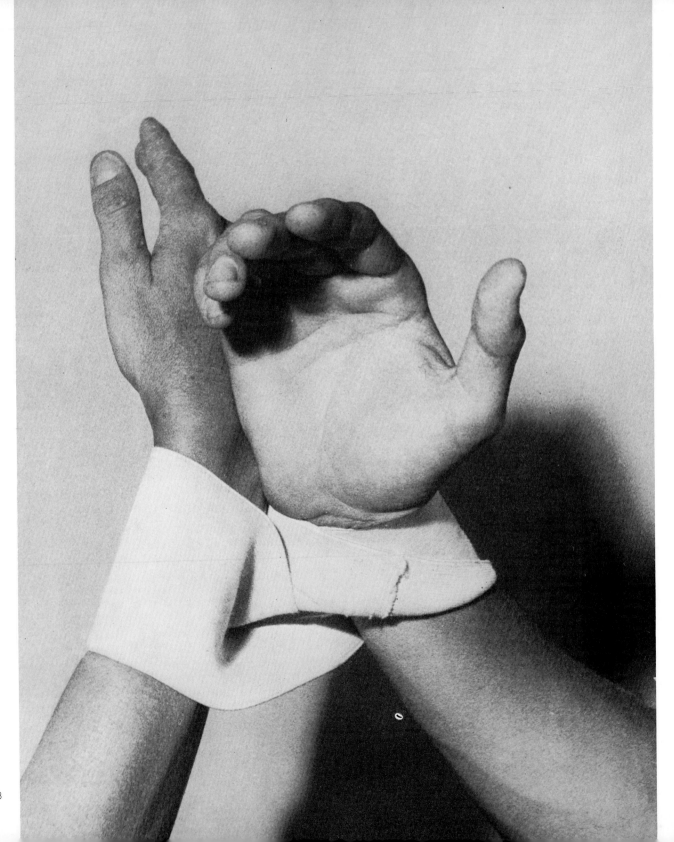

85

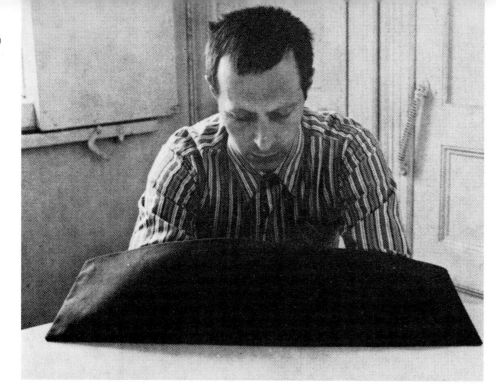

92

93

125

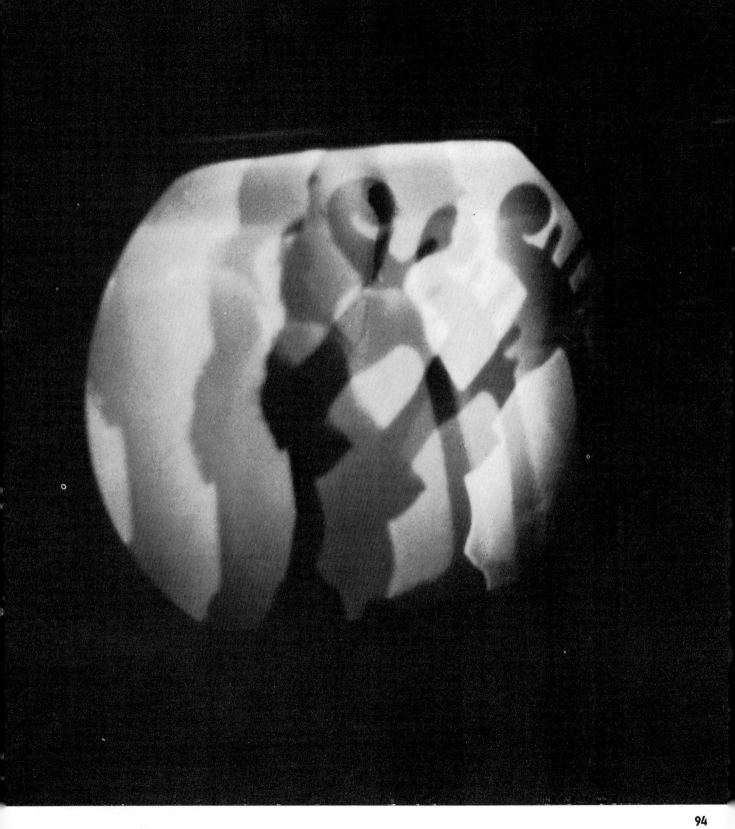

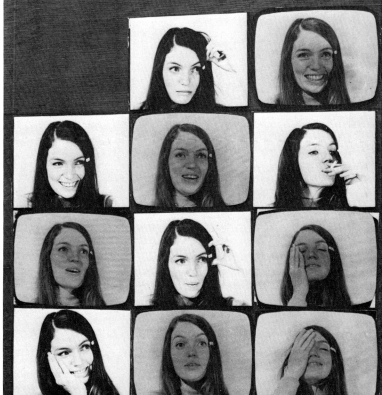

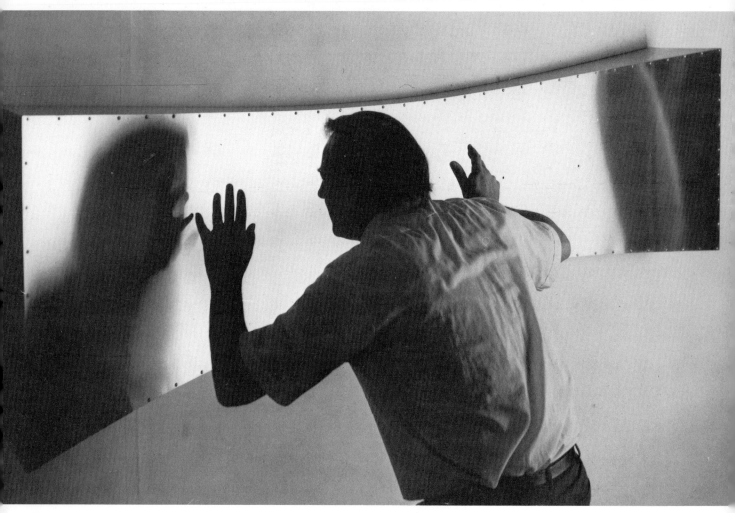

97

98

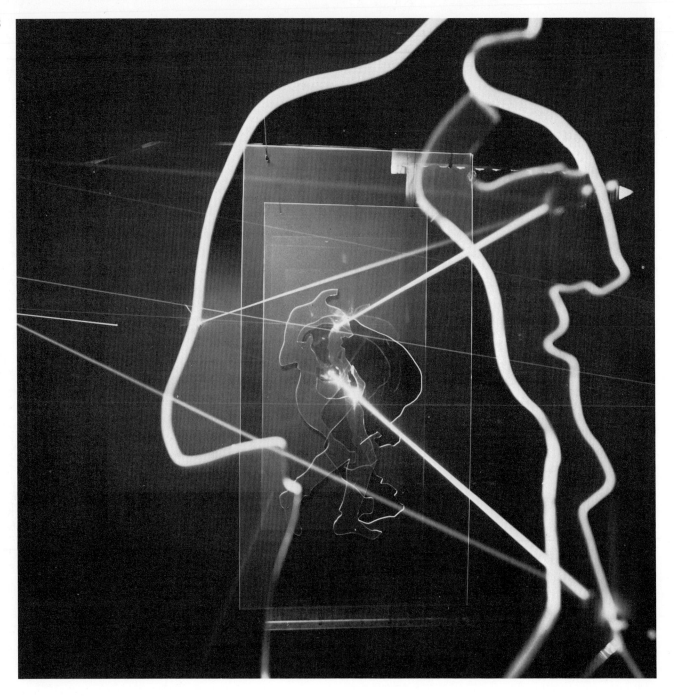

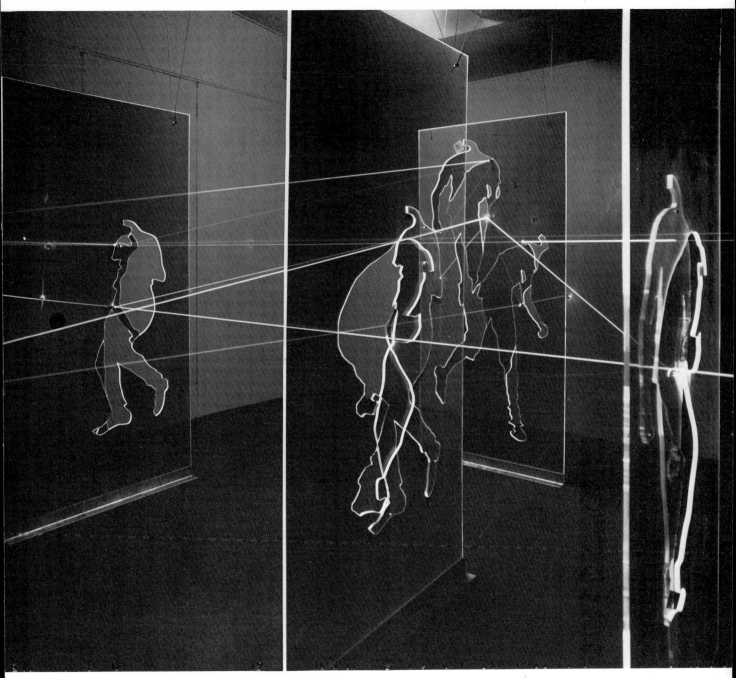

"Everything is metamorphosing."

Tetsumi Kudo

4 Because the reality of life has become more and more the main concern of culture in the broad sense, the accents have shifted from an art that is separate from life to one that concentrates on life in all its aspects. This process has brought basic human symbols and constants into the open—hidden, forgotten, or buried Ur-experiences that determine the elemental existence of man. The real, the elemental, life itself is allowed to speak for itself again—the opposite of an invented, metaphorical reality which only mental bridges serve to connect with life.

The decisive processes and events that determine the shape of our lives, from birth through sexual intercourse and love to death, have thus become artists' favored themes. They have found their expression in temporal sequences, in processes, actions, and ceremonies. These life processes are no longer being realized visually; they are being documented in as real a way as possible. Stan Brackhage, for instance, filmed the birth of his own children. He said that he was trying to destroy the myths of his childhood with "Scenes From Under Childhood": "A visualization of the inner world of fetal beginnings, the infant, the baby, the child—a shattering of the 'myths of childhood' through revelation of the extremes of violent terror and overwhelming joy of that world darkened to most adults by their sentimental remembering of it."

A second important period of every man's life, the transition from childhood to adulthood, is for the great majority of primitive peoples highly significant as a time for initiation.[81] Like primitive rituals, the most salient characteristic of contemporary Happenings is their ambivalence: death and life are interwoven into one process. The initiation rites among Australian aborigines

81   Bruno Bettelheim, Symbolic Wounds, London, 1955.

have three phases. First, the boys are covered with cloths and hidden from view to symbolize burial: their childhood has died. The circumcision ceremony is a sacrifice, an offering up of part of the human body (pars pro toto), again, the child is killed so the man might be born. After the operation the boys receive a huge penis as a symbol of their masculinity. Acceptance into the adult community is seen here as the birth of a new person. Sexuality, anchored in the religion of the fertility cult, is especially significant as a life-giving power.

Newer rites, such as graduation ceremonies, confirmation, or consecration have the same content—their purpose is to introduce the adolescent into the world of the adult and to give him the ability to stand on his own feet in it. But erotic love and sexuality are almost completely absent from these modern rites as a result of Christian teachings. Adolescents today are treated according to the generally accepted ethos of economic usefulness and readied in schools, universities and trade to take their places in the production process: they are treated one-dimensionally, as half-persons. Happenings, films, and theater productions, directed programmatically at sexual emancipation, are confronting this fact and trying their best to change it.

Love, eroticism, and sexuality play such a decisive role in contemporary life due, in great part, to the influence of Christianity.[82] Perhaps this represents subconscious compensation of the cult of fertility in a society that has and makes use of every opportunity to hinder fertility.

Sex in advertising, fashion, and entertainment is, like striptease dancing, symptomatic of sexuality robbed of its original function and become autonomous, a sexuality that corresponds to our time; that is, a sexuality absolutely legitimate and logical historically.

The Happenings of Otto Mühl, the actions and films of Carolee Schneeman, Iimura, Stan Brackhage, Jack Smith, George Kuchar, and Andy Warhol are, like the propositions of Yayoi Kusama, manifestations of this spirit. They all document the process of physical union. The flowering of erotic theater and numerous exhibitions of erotic art show that the taboos surrounding sexuality are being broken down.

Throughout the history of civilizations, rituals and taboos have also informed the lowly but life-giving process of eating. The film "Eat" (1964), by Andy Warhol, enabled us, with its unceasing observation, to see and become conscious once again of this process, similar to the way Gertrude Stein visualized the rose by repeating the word for it. Ann Halprin changed a banquet into a Happening, food plays an important role in Otto Mühl's "material actions," and Allan Kaprow created an "eat" environment. Claes Oldenburg achieved fascinating and shocking effects by identifying edibles with sex; Carolee Schneeman was interested in making the same connection. She wrote the

82 E. E. Goldsmith, Life Symbols as Related to Sex Symbols, London, 1924; E. Podolosky and C. Wade, Erotic Symbolism, New York, 1960; J. Evolva, Metaphysik des Sexus, Stuttgart, 1962.

following about her event "Meat Joy" (1964): "My kinetic theater provides for an intensification of all faculties simultaneously a mobile, tactile event into which the eye leads the body. I assume that senses crave sources of maximum information... 'Meat Joy,' a stifling vision now, relating Artaud, McClure, and French butcher shops, acting and viewing space interchanged. I see several girls whose gestures develop from a tactile, bodily relationship to individual men and to a mass of meat slices."[83]

Norman O. Brown writes in "Love's Body": "Eating is a form of sex copulation, is oral copulation. When the Aranda ask each other 'Have you eaten?' they mean 'Have you had intercourse?'"[84] Over a century ago Novalis evoked ideas like this with the question: "Is not an embrace similar to the evening meal?"

The association of ritual with things of the flesh is also embodied in the references to cannibalism one finds in modern art. Dali garnished a young girl ready for serving on a tray, Yves Klein entitled one of his large "anthropometries" "Grande Anthropophagie Bleue" and said: "Freedom in the original sense of its material, in short, life, specialized and edible for the finer senses."[85] Dali spoke of the edible beauty of Art Nouveau and the Yugoslav Adriano Spatola said "Poetry should be eaten and drunk." Like Claes Oldenburg, Joseph Beuys with his numerous events, his Fettbilder, Fettecken and Fettklötzen (literally, pictures made with fat, corners filled with fat, and simply lumps of fat), his chocolate bars painted brown, his potatoes and jelly beans, has developed an obsession with food which, layer after layer, has made us conscious of ancient rituals once more.

Today, as at all times in the past, the theme of death occupies a central position in art, supplemented by the perennial search for forms of life after death. It is a transition from one condition into another that is the artist's concern, into a condition that cannot be concretely experienced. Death and rebirth is a theme in art that has seen innumerable variations. In the 1960s the death theme was expressed in a very immediate way in Andy Warhol's early car crash paintings, his Marilyn Monroe series and the Kennedy pictures, and in his lapidary, documentary reproductions of electric chairs and atomic bomb explosions.

Paul Thek's sculpture in space "The Tomb" (1967) is an emotionally overwhelming variation on the old grave sculpture; it historicizes insofar as it copies ancient Egyptian burial chamber patterns and is contemporary in the authenticity of its vision. The fact that the artist has fashioned his own grave here may perhaps be interpreted as a sacrifice, a sacrifice of self to society. Keith Arnatt realized his "Self-Burial" (1969) as a ritual corresponding to the requirements of television.[86]

83 Richard Schechner, Public Domain, New York, 1969, p. 141.
84 Norman O. Brown, Love's Body, New York, 1966, p. 167. See also C. Strehlow, Die Aranda und Lovitja Stämme in Zentral Australien, Frankfurt, 1910.
85 Paul Wember, Yves Klein, Cologne, 1969, p. 50.
86 Catalogue of the TV Gallery Gerry Schum (Berlin), Cologne, 1970.

This theme appears again and again in films, plays, and Happenings. Stan Brackhage's "The Dead" (1960), Ed Emshwiller's "Thanatopsis" (1962), Stan VanDerBeek's anti-war film "Breathdeath" (1963–64), dedicated to Charlie Chaplin and Buster Keaton, Kenneth Anger's "Scorpio Rising" (1962–64), and Bruch Baillie's "Mass" (1964) all touch on the theme of death. In the productions the Performance Group has made to date, "Dionysos 69" and "Makbeth," death is the central motif.[87]

The burial ceremony played a role in Jean-Jacques Lebel's Happening "Cérémonie funèbre" (1960), an event that included the "death of the body," readings from the Marquis de Sade on love and death, masturbation, and as climax, a burial. Allan Kaprow presented his Happening "A Service for the Dead" in 1962; Hermann Nitsch's mutilation of lamb corpses shows his involvement with death. The final image of his Happenings is that of the artist himself, covered with blood, crucified—this, too, symbolizes a sacrifice of self to the society. Death and rebirth, metamorphosis, are the themes of Tetsumi Kudo's Happenings. He used the ritual form of suicide of his home country in the piece "Harakiri of Humanism," which can also be interpreted as self-sacrifice for the good of the many.

However, all these activities of contemporary artists were eclipsed totally by a series of events that spoke to the emotions of the masses much more directly—the incidents of public self-immolation, a ritual offering up of the self to society in an era when the old rituals are losing more and more of their meaning. Real events are related in this way to the works and actions of contemporary artists, occupy the same sphere of effect and share a ritual intensity.

 87 Richard Schechner, Public Domain, New York, 1969.

109

111

112

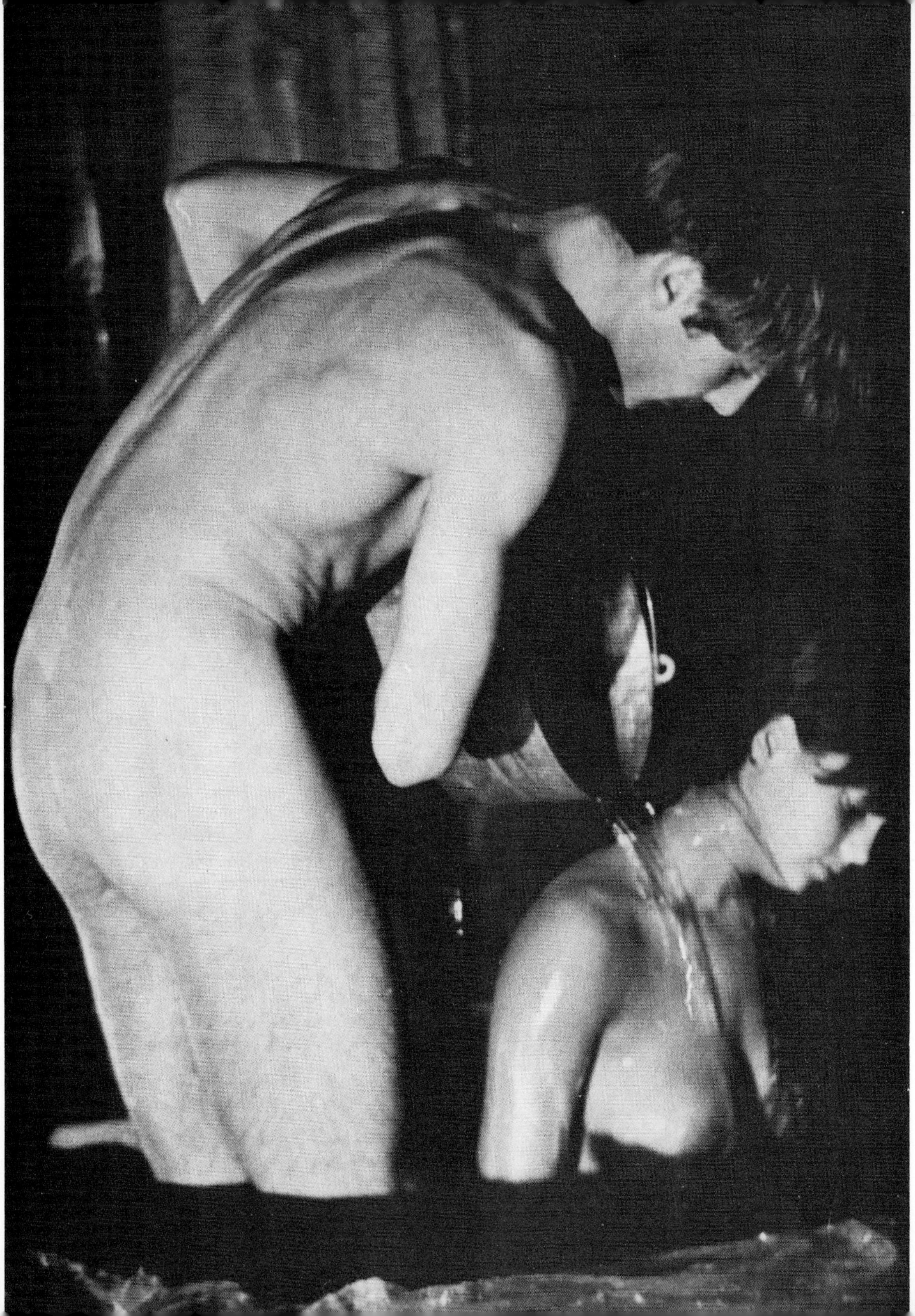

114

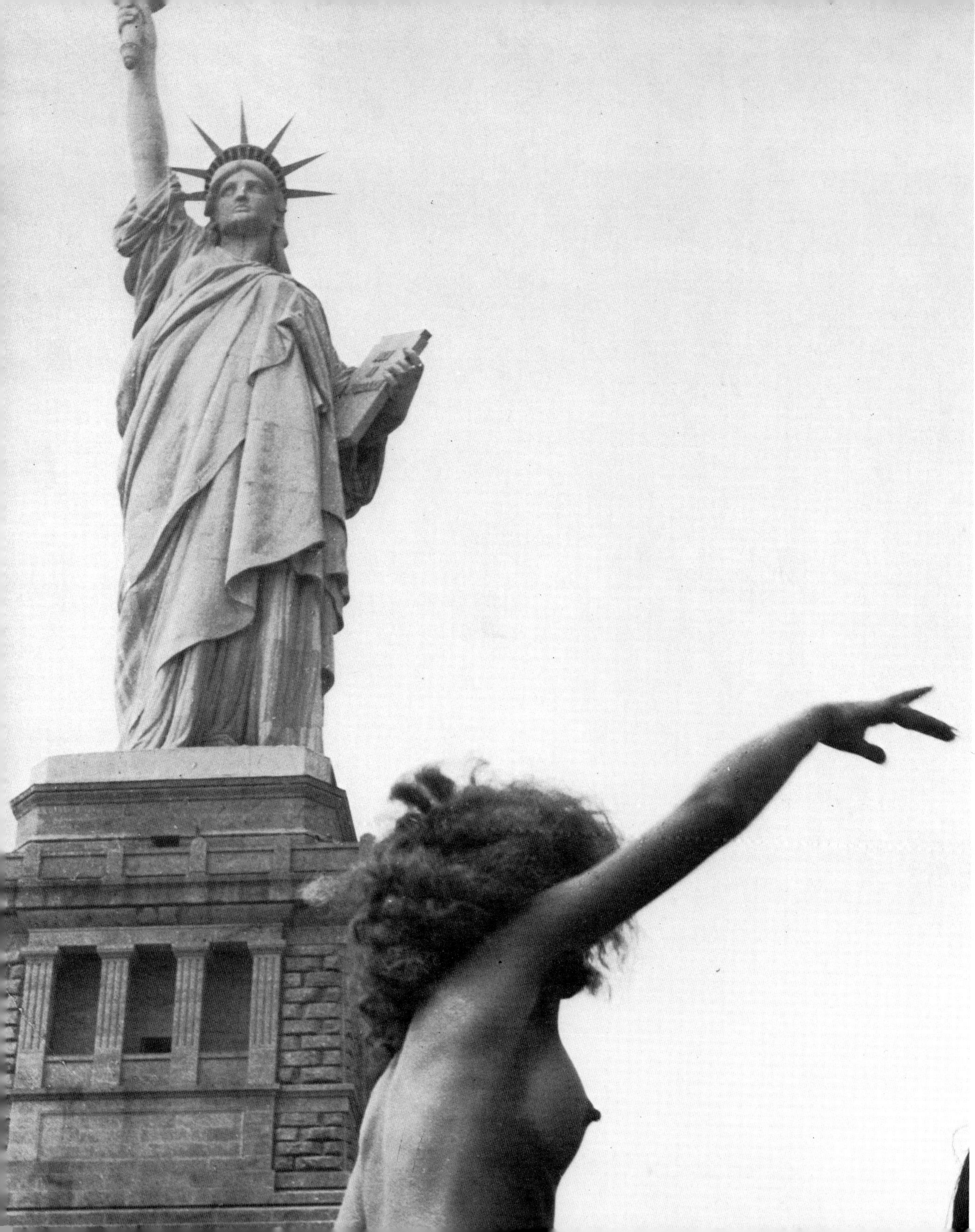

118

119

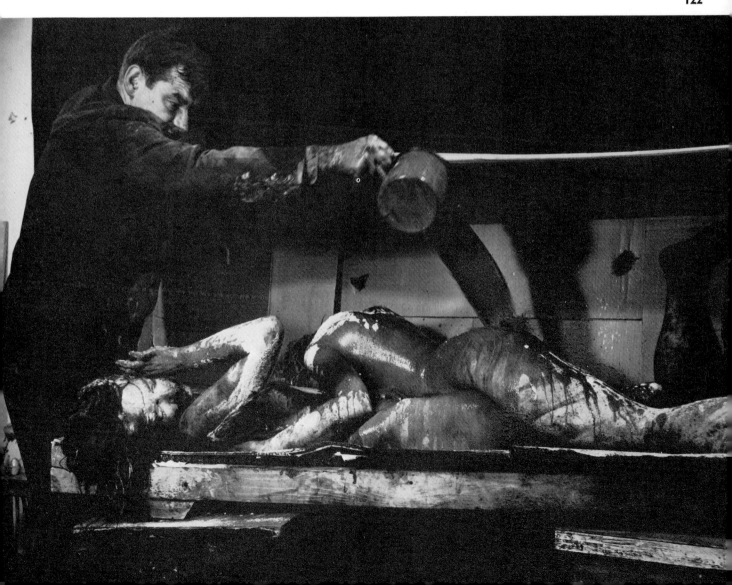

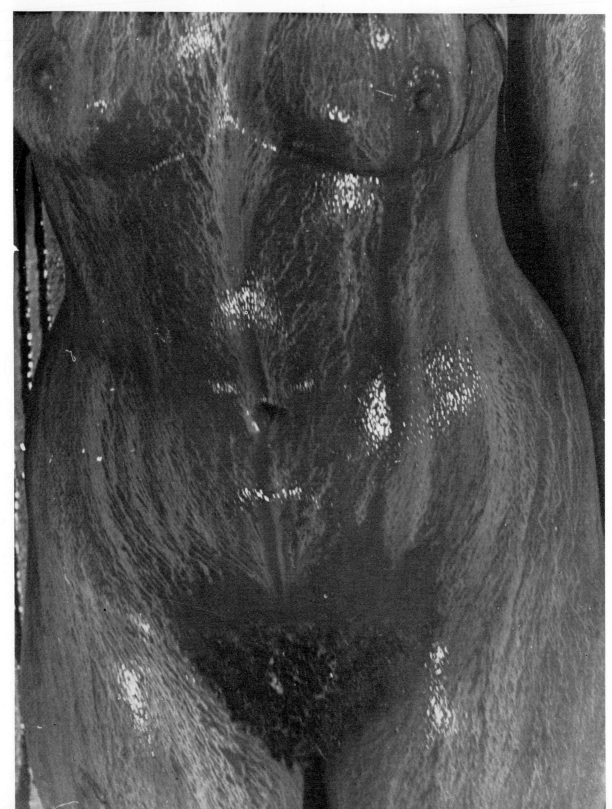

124

EINLADUNG ZUR ERÖFFNUG DIENSTAG DEN 1. JULI 20 UHR FALLMEREYERSTR. 28

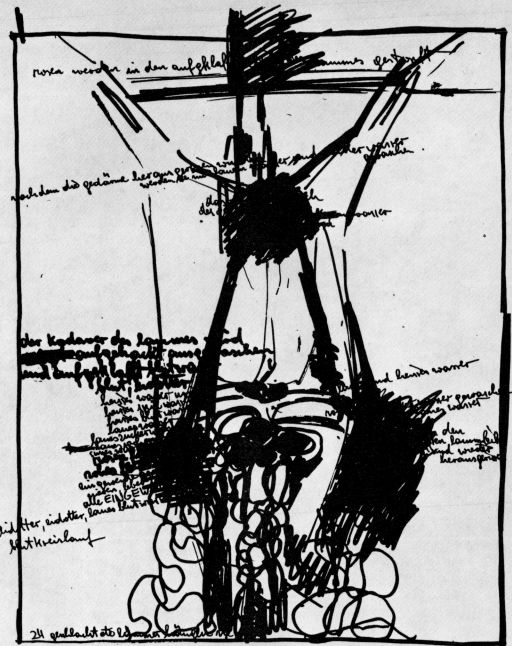

NITSCH

AVANT ART GALERIE CASA ZEIGT **DOKUMENTATIONEN** ZUM **O.M. THEATER**
TEXTE-PARTITUREN-SKIZZEN-FOTOS UND POLIZEIBERICHTE
VOM 1.–15. JULI 1969 · MONTAG–FREITAG 14–20 UHR
IN DEN RÄUMEN DER GALERIE NEUHAUS MÜNCHEN · FALLMEREYERSTRASSE 28

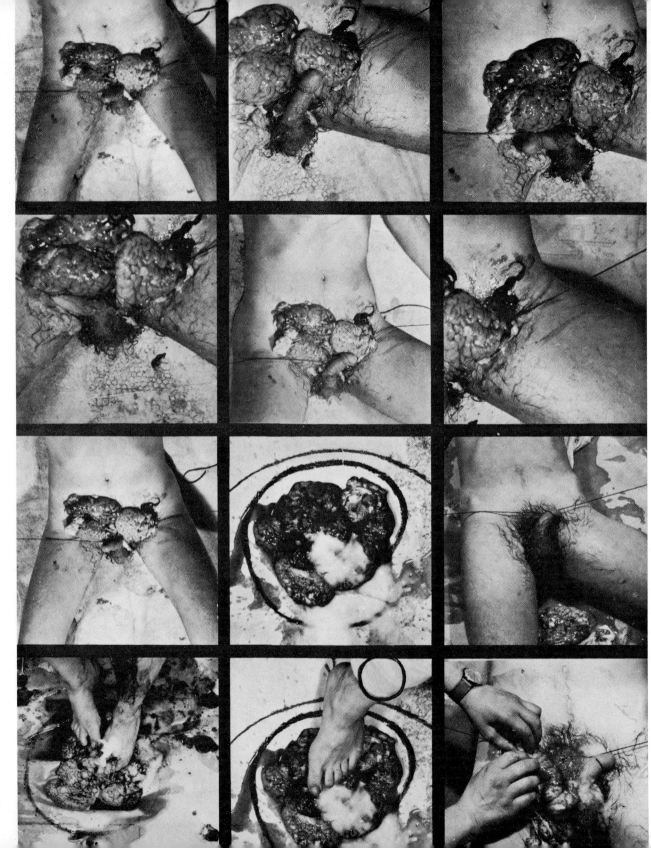

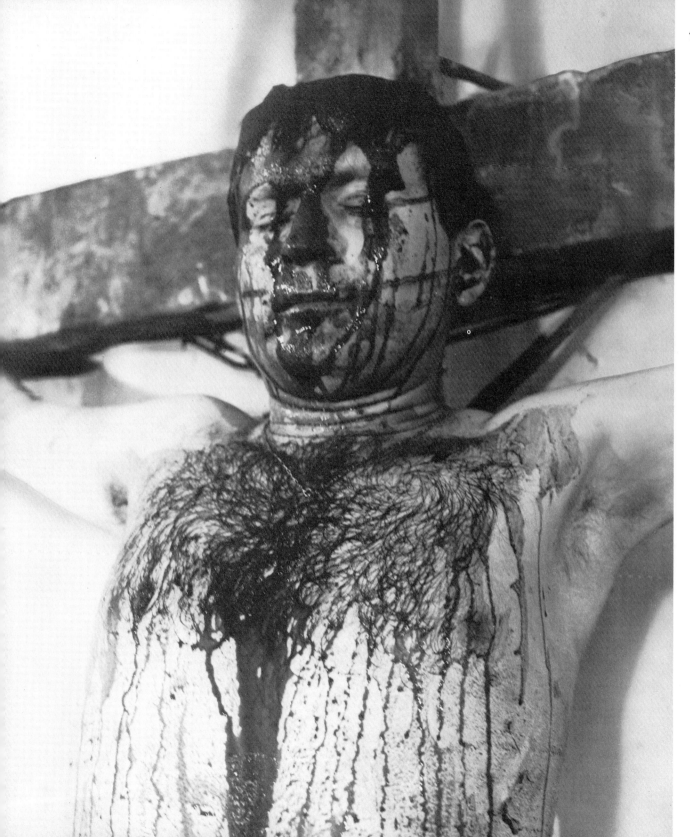

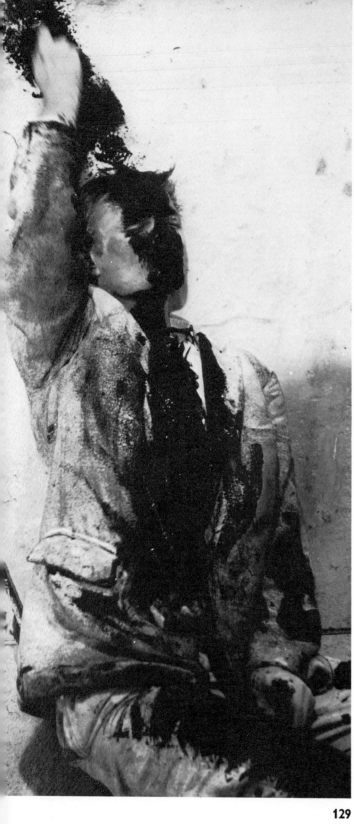

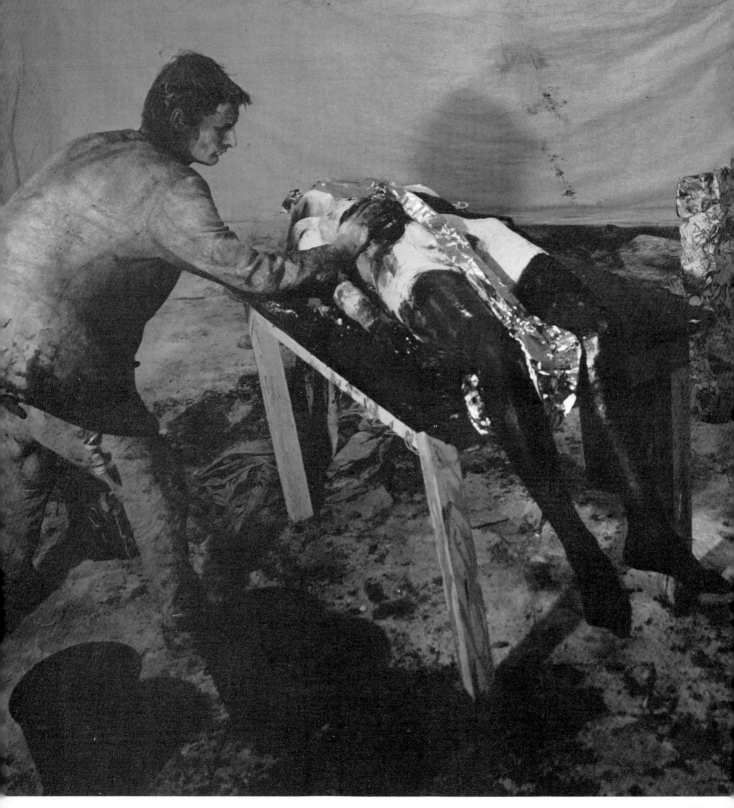

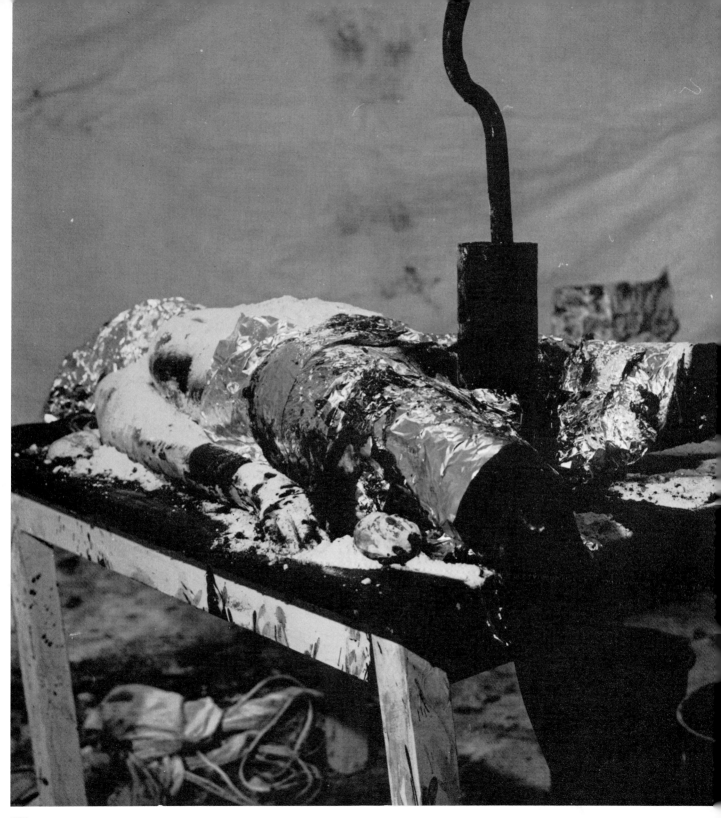

134

135

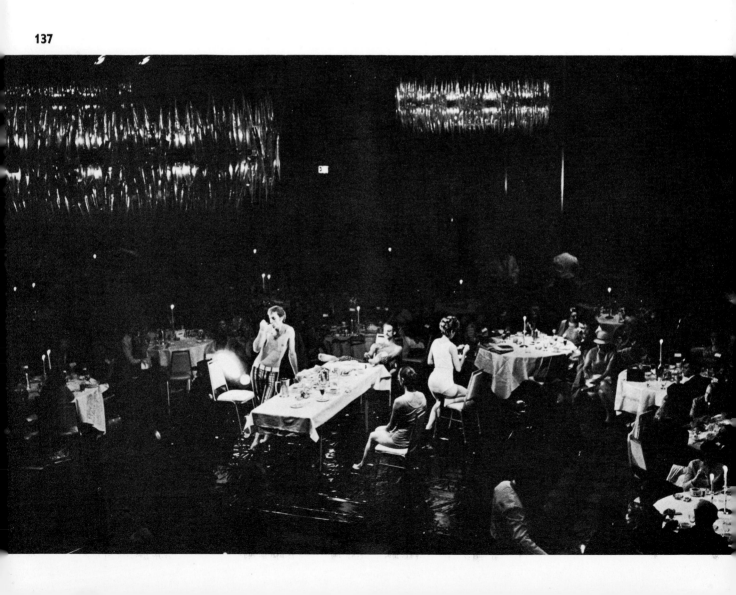

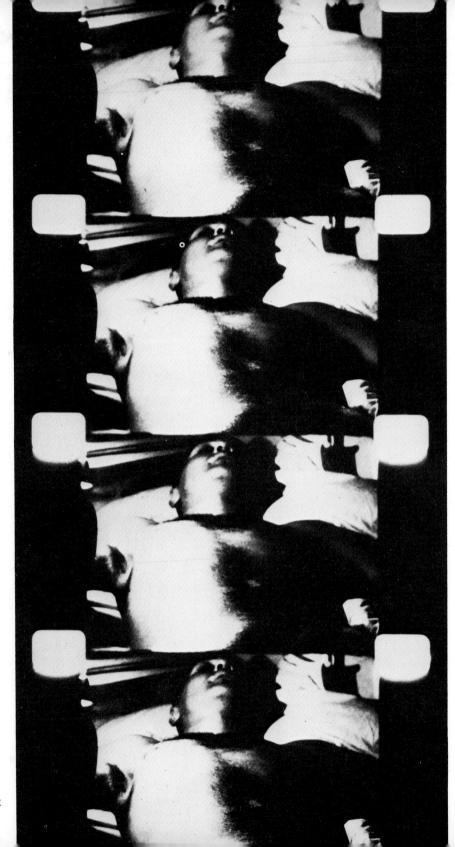

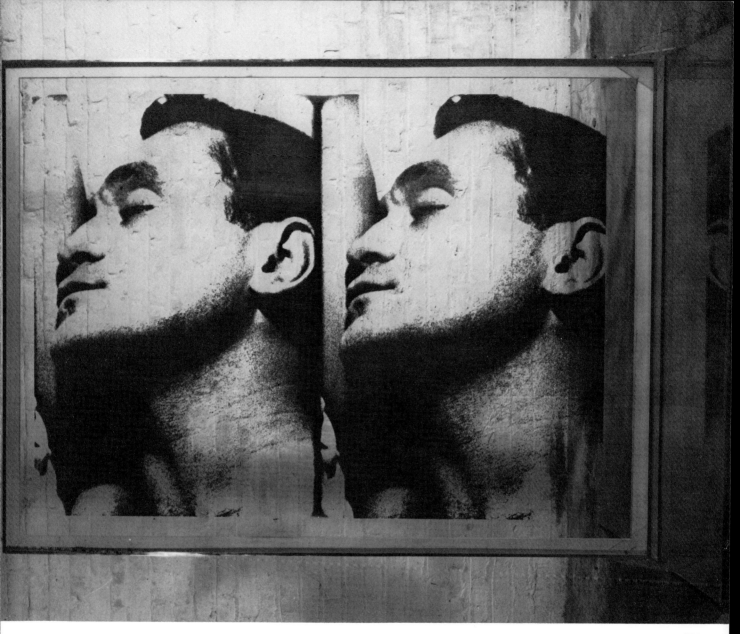

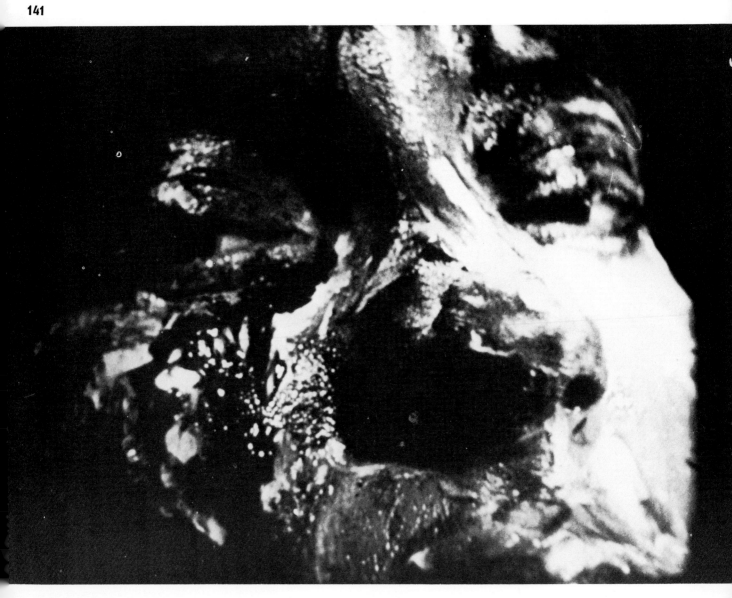

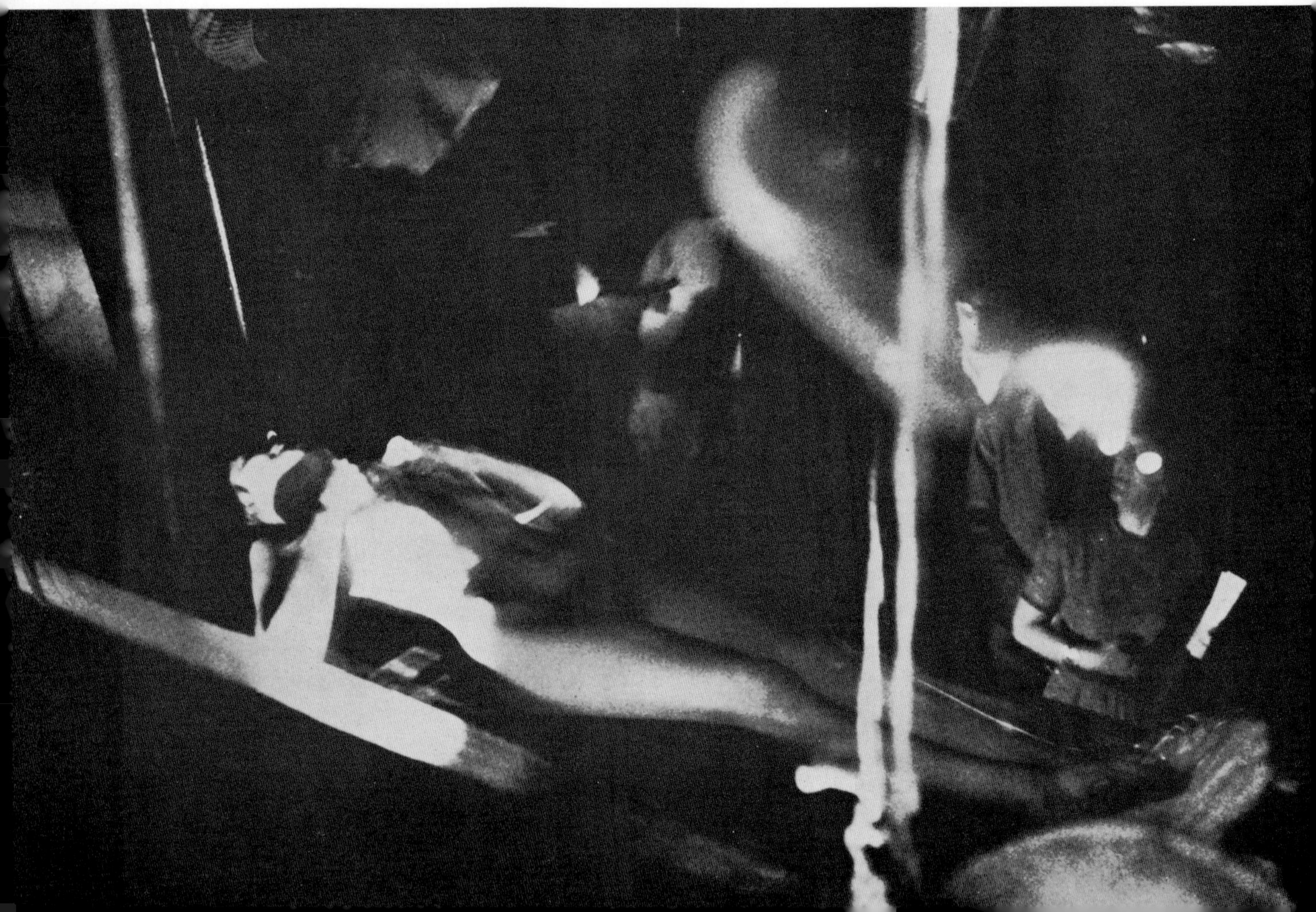

145

"The visible world is no longer a reality and the unseen
world is no longer a dream."

William Butler Yeats

5 "There is no 'gap' between art and life" (Rafael Ferrer). This feeling, given
expression by many contemporary artists, is especially apt for the art that
alters and transforms our world on a large scale (at least in conception) and
is called variously land art, arte povera, and conceptual art.[88] The artists
working in this field are also centrally concerned with showing us that art
and life are really one.

Today the basic, elemental events in nature and life are once more so important that natural processes have become part of a creative activity that includes both life and art. Historic predecessors for this elemental approach
include perhaps the grave of the Emperor Mintoku near Osaka in whose
design earth plays the key role,[89] the huge earth drawings in southern Peru,
and the pictures the Navaho Indians still paint with sand. Navaho art is made
up largely of circles and closed forms with mandala character that symbolize a living whole and are meant either to create or reconstruct a whole person capable of life. Mandalas are supposed to restore disturbed balance—that
is, to heal sickness, which is considered by the Indians to be an imbalance in
the organism. Mental disturbances can be healed through meditation, by
pondering the balanced order of a healthy whole.

The activities of young artists that create direct connections to earth, the elements, sand, cliffs, trees, stones, rock formations under the surface of the

88 Germano Celant, Art Povera; New York, 1969, catalogue of the TV exhibition "Land
Art," TV Gallery Gerry Schum (Berlin), Cologne, 1969.
89 M. Suenaga, Old Tombs from the Air, Tokyo, 1955; M. Suenaga, A. Shimada, and D.
Harada, Japanese Old Tomb Sculpture, Tokyo, 1954.

earth and on the sea's floor are similarly concerned with restoring the psychic balance of man, because time and processes occuring over a period of time have such an important place in their work. The growth and ripening of crops, the ebb and flow of the tides, natural processes where one has to deal with cosmic intervals, functions man has learned to know well over thousands of years on earth—these are used by artists today to induce us to meditate and, through meditation, to restore our relationship to reality.

Numerous artists, working both indoors and out, have conceived projects that follow the rules of nature and use natural materials, natural elements, natural processes and, often, time itself. Rafael Ferrer's work is a search to find ways for materials from nature to be aesthetically effective in themselves or in combination with materials produced by technology. In autumn he uses fallen leaves, in summer hay, in winter chunks of ice; he uses these materials to create forms suggested by the internal laws of each substance. The result is freedom, a new interaction of authentic materials and systems of laws, a new position with respect to reality.

Jan Dibbets has combined ponds of water, tape recorders, branches, and grass in (indoor) space. In Forest Piece (Giles Strut Bridge, Ithaca, New York, 1969), he went one step further and began altering nature on site. He selectively painted tree trunks white in order to introduce dimension and suggest direction in nature—parameters it otherwise lacks. The "trail through the woods" thus created is of unlimited size; its dimensions are arbitrary. "The Forest" was the title of a Happening done by Allan Kaprow in 1962 in which the participants represented a forest, each one a tree or bush, that moved.

Robert Morris, in his "Los Angeles Project II" (1969), would like to change the climate of an entire region with the help of computer technology. He chose Rembrandt's etching "Three Trees" on which to base his sketch for the project; it is to be realized on a square mile of landscape with vegetation. Morris wrote: "A site will be selected somewhere in Southern California. Buried underground within this area will be a number of large air conditioners and heaters of the type used in the ground support phase of ICBM technology. The outputs of hot and cold air will be above ground and disguised. In general, there will be a little more weather in the area after the project is completed. One could wander around and come upon these local changes of temperature—a cold wind blowing out of an otherwise still tree, or stones radiating heat, for example. Ecologic recordings will continue at all levels after installation of the technology with a view toward determining the changes which the artificial localized weather might produce on any aspect of the environment."[90]

Carl Andre, known mainly for his concrete paving stones which can be arranged in any desired pattern, placed a row of haystacks on a field near a woods in his piece Joint (1968). Richard Long created a series of earth mounds, often

90 Robert Morris, Ecologic Art, Los Angeles Project II, Summer, 1969.

circular or square, which remind one of the mandala forms of the Navajo Indians.

Barry Flanagan's "Hole in the Sea" (1969) consists of a Plexiglas cylinder sunk into the sand of a beach. As it slowly disappears under the rising water, one can experience in a very meditative way the otherwise imperceptible tide changes, ebb and flow. Peter Hutchinson goes directly into the environment of the sea floor and changes it as he wishes; the sculptures "Arc" and "Threaded Calabash" (both 1969) are good examples of his work.

Other regions contemporary artists find irresistible are the desert (Walter de Maria: "Wall in the Desert," 1968 and "Two Lines Three Circles on the Desert," 1969; Mike Heizer: "Coyote," 1969), the landscape of the Camargue (Marinus Boezem: "Sand Fountain," 1969), quarries, snowscapes, and coastlines. After the exclusively big city orientation of the past decades in art, nature has been rediscovered, re-interpreted, and utilized as a stimulus to the emotions. Once before, in the 1920s and around 1930, artists went "into the desert" (D. H. Lawrence, Max Ernst, Frank Lloyd Wright); all were looking for an elemental environment suited to their artistic intentions. Experiencing nature through the senses is something the artist has made possible for us at a point in time when man has triumphed over nature to such an extent that he is capable of leaving the planet.

Land art has nothing to do with an escape from the dying city. Many of its creators are products of the big city and want to stay that way. They go at nature with all the means technology has put at their disposal. That they are deeply concerned with reaffirming the authenticity of the natural, with its cosmic patterns, is shown by the work of Dennis Oppenheim, who, with his "Time Line" on the American-Canadian border, has visualized an abstract, geographic schema and made it intelligible to all the senses. "Weather Data Plotted on Bean Field" and "Directed Seeding-Wheat" (both 1969) are also conceived along these lines; in the second piece the dimension of time joins the other three in covering a great area, for the growth of wheat takes not only space, it takes time, a lot of it. This time is one of the parameters of the work.

The time factor plays a comparable role in the products of Peter Hutchinson. His glass tubes, destined for such places as Mauna Loa in Hawaii ("Edge of Active Volcano," 1969), Greenland ("Iceberg Project," 1969), and Storm King Mountain, New York (1969), are designed to confront nature's processes of change with the processes of decay—also a form of change—that take place inside them. His Plexiglas containers are filled with algae, earth, and chemicals that change continually.

Real alterations of the earth's surface on a huge scale have been Christo's preoccupation for a long time. In 1968–69 in Little Bay, near Sidney, Australia, he had the chance to realize his work "Packed Coast." He wrapped a million square feet of rocky coastline in plastic sheeting.

These few examples show the possibilities and visions of an art that makes use of the elemental and the cosmic. The contemporary nature of this art is underlined by the fact that it can be achieved only with the help of the most modern technology; often, works in this genre can be seen only from the air, or they are expressly conceived for television.

The dimensions of this art point to the unbelievable expansion of our world of experience. As early as 1961 Piero Manzoni put the world on a pedestal ("Socle du Monde").[91] In May of 1969 Marinus Boezem had the idea of signing the universe with the help of an airplane whose condensation trails would spell out his name. "That which is boundless is greatest," said Paul Scheerbart, "but that which is boundless is infinite space, the universe. We no longer want to exist separate from it."[92] Man had to wait until the second half of the 20th century to experience the universe; it now belongs to his environment. It is no longer heaven, to be prayed to and worshipped, and it is no longer matter to be grasped in the abstract—it is physical experience.

91 Exhibition catalogue, "Piero Manzoni, " Eindhoven Museum (1969); Monchen–Gladbach Museum (1970); Stedelijk Museum, Amsterdam (1970).
92 Udo Kultermann, "Paul Scheerbart und die Architektur im 20. Jahrhundert," in Handbuch des Bauwesens, Stuttgart, 1963.

149

152

153

154

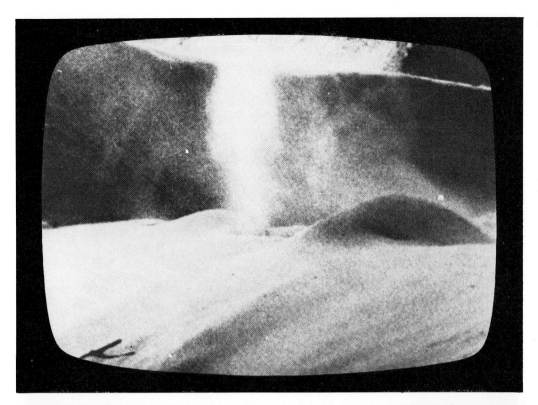

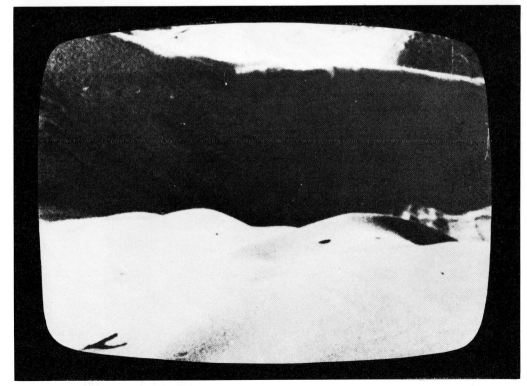

157

For Lucille

LOS ANGELES PROJECT. II

April Green Landscape ?

Typical Units →

All devices buried underground

Outputs above ground

159

160

Nebraska Project

SIZE: 300' x 1000'
MEDIA: CULTIVATOR TRACTOR ON UN-SEEDED FIELD.
SUBJECT: CONTOUR LINES TAKEN FROM QUADRANGLE MAP OF NORTHERN WISCONSIN ENLARGED AND PLOTTED ON LAND.

163

198

164

165

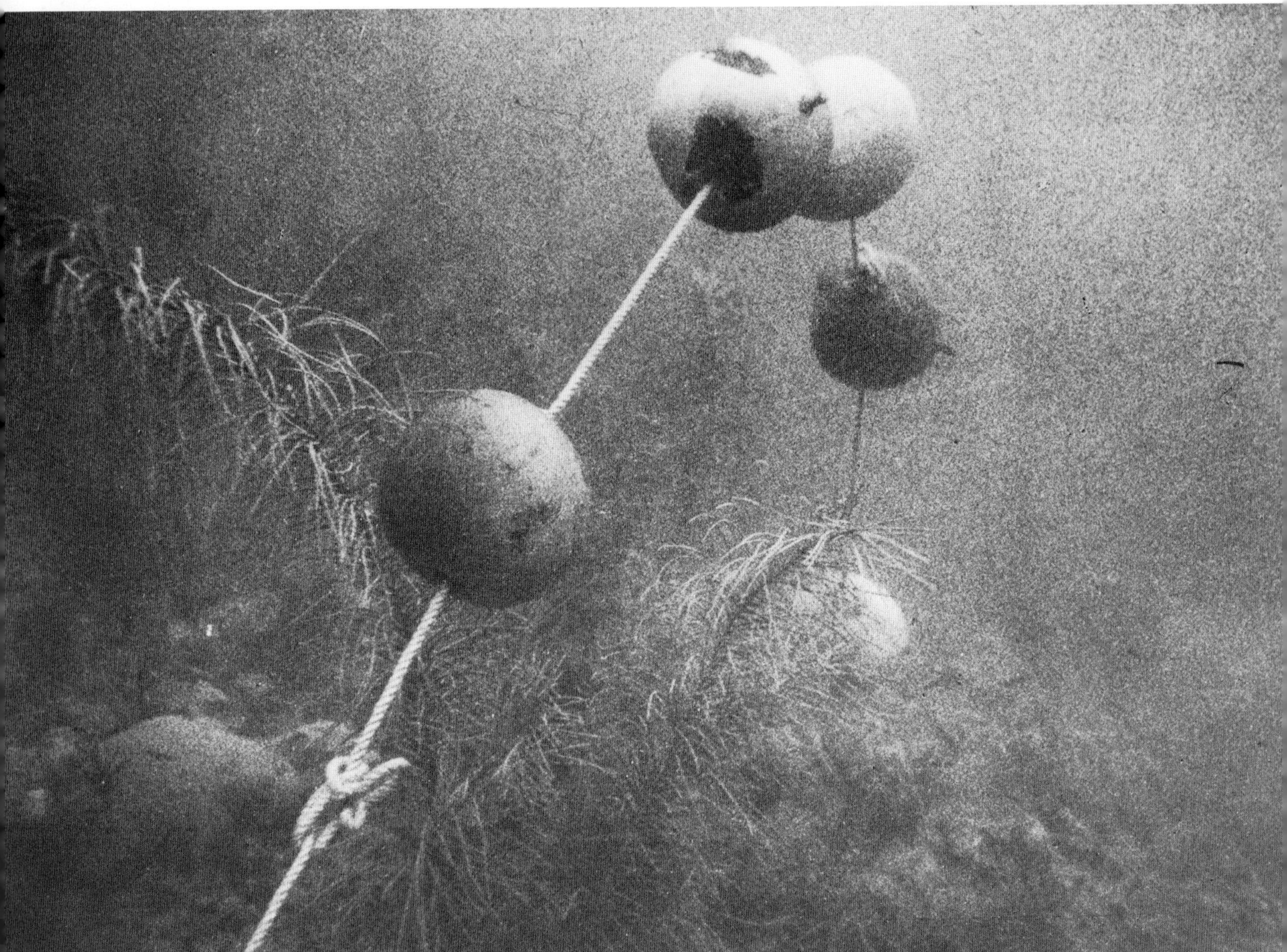

168

169

COAST (PROJECT FOR AUSTRALIA NEAR SYDNEY - LITTLE BAY - SURFACE AREA 300000 SQ AND FEET) Christo 1969

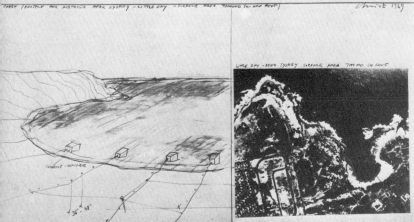

LITTLE BAY - NEAR SYDNEY SURFACE AREA 700,000 SQ FEET

171

172

"We don't need laws, we need feelings."

Julian Beck

Conclusion   "Imagination takes command"—this is the demand, based on a general desire, especially on the part of the younger generation, to rebuild the community from the ground up. The prerequisite is personal responsibility. Art, above all art that takes the form of open-ended, unplanned Happenings, plays an important role in this process. Varieties of experience that transcend knowledge are decisive. Artists, rejection of a materialistic point of view all over the world indicates a growing trust in psychic, magical, and mythic values. Everything is related to everything else, it's "all in the same bag." These interrelationships are not static, they are continually in the process of becoming.[93] The circulation of the blood, electric current, sexual and cosmic interpenetration, intellectual, physical, emotional, and mythic insights flow together into a new, human system of values, an ethics based upon love and mutual help, the sign of a new epoch. The culture of the 1960s shows the way.

93   Norbert Weiner, Cybernetics; Tetsumi Kudo, Circuit; Reich, Theory of the Orgasm; Claes Oldenburg, Soft World.

Bob Altman, New York 18
Associated Press, London 2, 8, 9, 16
Ay-O, New York 77
Oscar Bailey, New York 55, 56
Barry Le Va, Minneapolis 150
Rudy Bender, San Francisco 87
Bewegungstheater Bewth, Amsterdam 37, 59, 61
Davide Boriani, Rome 100
Stan Brakhage, Arizona 121
Günter Brus, Vienna 129, 130, 131, 132, 133
Rudolph Burckhardt, New York 136
Leo Castelli, New York 136, 139, 140, 158
Cimaise, Paris 18
Luigi Ciminaghi, Milan 66
Lygia Clark, Paris 78, 79, 80, 81, 82, 83
Colby Junior College, New London, New Hampshire 72
The Cunningham Dance Foundation, New York 55, 56
Jan Dibbets, Amsterdam 151
Horace Dimayo 111, 112
Jean Dupuy, Paris 105, 106
Stephan Dwoskin, London 141
Ed Emshwiller, New York 53, 142
Erro, Paris 52
Rafael Ferrer, Philadelphia 148
Galerie Hans Neuendorf, Hamburg 90, 91
Geiger, Turin 24, 69
John Gibson, New York 72, 73, 74, 161, 162, 166, 167, 168, 170, 171
Piero Gilardi, Turin 93
Maria Gilissen, Antwerp 109
Hans Haacke, New York 99
Ann Halprin, San Francisco 70, 71, 84, 85, 86, 87, 89, 113, 138
Hanlor, Paris 75, 76
Robert Israel, New York 26
Istituto di Tella, Buenos Aires 119
Kaare Per Johannesen, Copenhagen 110
Howard Jones, St. Louis 97, 98
Kaiser Wilhelm Museum, Krefeld 1
Allan Kaprow, Glen Cove, New York 27, 28, 30, 35, 88, 114, 115, 143, 144
Bob Kline, San Francisco 70
Milan Knizak, Prague 43, 44, 45, 46
Volker Krämer, Düsseldorf 7
Tetsumi Kudo, Paris 39, 40, 41, 42, 111, 112

Yayoi Kusama, New York 118
Peter Kuttner, London 47, 135
Murray Louis, New York 54
Thomas Lüttge, Munich 5
Bob Machover, San Francisco 84
Klaus Medau, Düsseldorf 6
Gustav Metzger 31
John Milaire, New York 73
Martha Minujin, New York 101, 102
Charlotte Moorman, New York 67
André Morain, Paris 75, 76
Otto Mühl, Vienna 63, 120, 122, 123, 124
Osamu Murai, Tokyo 103, 104
Museum of Contemporary Art, Chicago 89
Museum Mönchen-Gladbach 20, 173
Hans Namuth, Düsseldorf 57
Hermann Nitsch, Munich 125, 126, 127, 128
Lufti Özkök, Stockholm 58
Nam June Paik, New York 67, 94
Nicholas Peckham, San Francisco 85, 86
The Performance Group, New York 38, 145, 146
Eric Pollitzer, Garden City, New York 140
Dölf Preisig, Zürich 50
Pressens Bild, Stockholm 51
Heinrich Riebesehl, Hannover 33, 34
David van Riper, Chicago 89
Paul Ryan, New York 89, 95, 96
Bob Sabin, New York 117
Anthony Scott, London 92
Shunk-Kender, New York 4, 149, 152, 158, 163, 164, 165, 169, 172
Howard Smagula, New York 74
Paolo Scheggi, Milan 65, 66
Alfred Schmela, Düsseldorf 57, 58
Carolee Schneemann, London 116
Gerry Schum, Berlin 147, 153, 154, 155, 156, 160
Aldo Tambellino, New York 32, 101
Atsuko Tanaka, Osaka 25
Joseph Tandl, Vienna 3
Thomas Tol, Amsterdam 37, 59, 61
Abisag Tüllmann, Frankfurt 107, 108
Keiji Usami, Tokyo 103, 104
Wide White Space Gallery, Antwerp 109